Heights Heights are given in metres or in feet above the charted height datum; details are given in the Explanatory Notes under the chart title. The position of a height is normally that of the dot alongside it, thus ·79. Parentheses are used when the figure expressing height is set apart from the object (eg when showing the height of a small islet). Clearance heights may be referred to a higher datum than other heights. In such cases this will be stated in the Explanatory Notes.

Bearings Bearings are given from seaward and refer to the true compass.

Sea Miles and Cables A sea mile is the length of one minute of latitude locally, and is the principal means of expressing distance on Admiralty charts. A cable is one-tenth of a sea mile.

Names Names on Admiralty charts are spelt in accordance with the principles and systems approved by the Permanent Committee on Geographical Names for British Official Use.

A second name may be given, usually in parentheses, in the following circumstances:
 a. if the retention of a superseded rendering will facilitate cross-reference to related publications;
 b. if, in the case of a name that has changed radically, the retention of the former one will aid recognition;
 c. if it is decided to retain an English conventional name in addition to the present official rendering;

Chart Catalogues Details of Admiralty charts are given in the "Catalogue of Admiralty Charts and Publications" (NP 131) and regional catalogues 'Caribbean' (NP105), 'Mediterranean' (NP106). 'Scandinavian' (NP107), 'North West Europe' (NP109), all published annually.

The Mariner's Handbook and other Publications The Mariner's Handbook (NP 100) includes information on the following:

The use of charts and the degree of reliance that may be placed on them; chart supply and correction; names; charted navigational aids; navigational hazards; traffic separation schemes; offshore oil and gas operations; tides and currents; general marine meteorology. A glossary of terms used on Admiralty charts is also given.

Information about features represented on charts can also be found in the following publications or their digital equivalents:

Admiralty Sailing Directions; Admiralty List of Lights and Fog Signals; Admiralty Tide Tables and Tidal Stream Atlases; Admiralty List of Radio Signals; Annual Notices to Mariners; IALA Maritime Buoyage System.

Copyright Admiralty charts and publications (including this one) are protected by Crown Copyright. They are derived from Crown Copyright information and from copyright information published by other organisations. They may not be reproduced in any material form (including photocopying or storing by electronic means) without prior permission of the copyright owners, which may be sought by applying, in the first instance, to the Copyright Manager; The United Kingdom Hydrographic Office, Taunton, Somerset TA1 2DN, UK.

A   Chart Number, Title, Marginal Notes

Schematic Layout of an Admiralty INT chart (reduced in size)

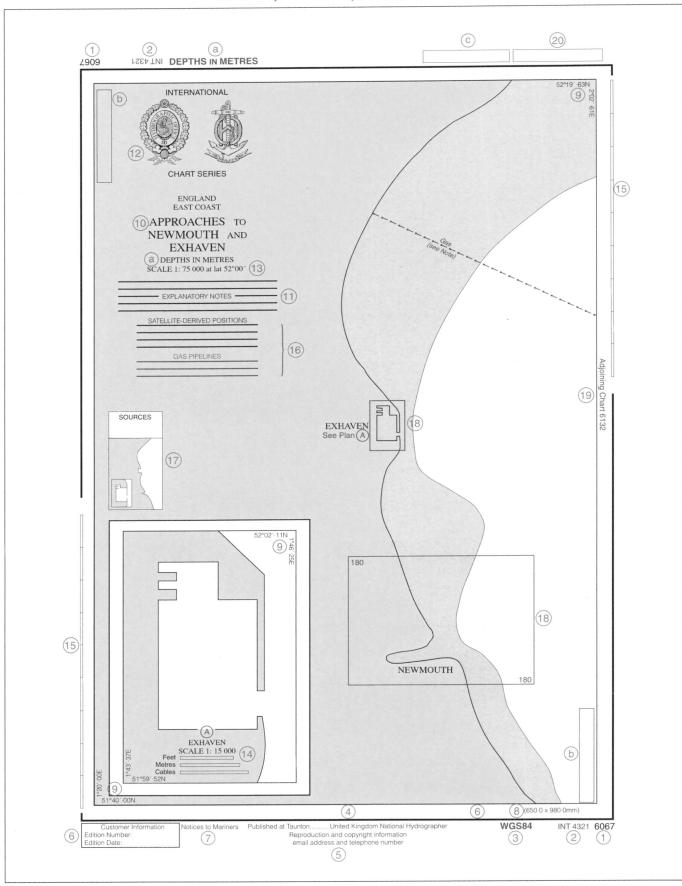

① 6067   ② INT 4321   ⓐ **DEPTHS IN METRES**   ⓒ   ⑳

52°19´·63N
2°02´·61E   ⑨

⑮

INTERNATIONAL

⑫

CHART SERIES

ENGLAND
EAST COAST

⑩ APPROACHES TO
NEWMOUTH AND
EXHAVEN

ⓐ DEPTHS IN METRES
SCALE 1: 75 000 at lat 52°00´   ⑬

———— EXPLANATORY NOTES ————   ⑪

SATELLITE-DERIVED POSITIONS

GAS PIPELINES   ⑯

Gas
(see Note)

SOURCES

⑰

Adjoining Chart 6132

⑲

EXHAVEN
See Plan ⓐ   ⑱

52°02´·11N
1°46´·25E   ⑨

180

⑱

NEWMOUTH

180

⑮

ⓐ
EXHAVEN
SCALE 1: 15 000   ⑭
Feet
Metres
Cables
51°59´·52N

1°43´·37E

1°20´·00E
⑨
51°40´·00N

ⓑ

④   ⑥   ⑧ (650·0 x 980·0mm)

Customer Information
⑥ Edition Number:
Edition Date:
⑦ Notices to Mariners   Published at Taunton..........United Kingdom National Hydrographer
Reproduction and copyright information
email address and telephone number   ⑤

WGS84   ③   INT 4321 ②   6067 ①

4

| Magnetic Features → B | Tidal Data → H | Satellite Navigation Systems → S |

1. Chart number in the Admiralty series.

251

2. Chart number in the International (INT) Chart series.

251.1

3. Use of WGS84 geodetic reference system.

201
255.3

4. Publication note (imprint) showing the date of publication as a New Chart.

252.1
252.4

5. Reproduction and Copyright acknowledgement note. All Admiralty charts are subject to Crown Copyright restrictions.

253

6. Customer Information, Edition Number, Edition Date, (charts revised prior to May 2000 have New Edition date at bottom right of chart)

252.2

7. Notices to Mariners: (a) the year dates and numbers of Notices to Mariners and (b) the dates (usually bracketed) of minor corrections included in reprints but not formally promulgated (abandoned as a method of correction in 1986), (charts revised prior to May 2000 have the legend 'Small corrections').

252.3

8. Dimensions of the inner neat-lines of the chart border. In the case of charts on Transverse Mercator and Gnomonic projections, dimensions may be quoted for all borders of the chart which differ. Some Fathoms charts show the dimensions in inches e.g. (38.40 x 25.40).

222.3
222.4

9. Corner co-ordinates.

214

10. Chart title. This should be quoted, in addition to the chart number, when ordering a chart.

241.3

11. Explanatory notes on chart content; **to be read before using the chart**.

242

12. Seals. Where an Admiralty chart is in the International Chart series, the seal of the International Hydrographic Organization (IHO) is shown in addition to the national seal. Reproductions of international charts of other nations (facsimile) have the seals of the original producer (left), publisher (centre) and the IHO (right). Reproductions of other charts have the seals of original producer (left) and publisher (right); charts which are co-productions carry the seals of the nations involved in their production.

241.1
241.2

13. Scale of chart; on Mercator projection, at a stated latitude.

211
241.4

14. Linear scales on large-scale plan.

221

15. Linear border scales (metres). On smaller scale charts, the latitude border should be used to measure Sea miles and Cables.

221.1

16. Cautionary notes (if any) on charted detail; **to be read before using the chart**.

242

17. Source Diagram (if any). If a Source Diagram is not shown, details of the sources used in the compilation of the chart are given in the explanatory notes (see 10). **The Source Diagram or notes should be studied carefully before using the chart in order to assess the reliability of the sources**.

290-298

18. Reference to a larger scale chart or plan (with reference letter if plan on same chart).

254

19. Reference to an adjoining chart of similar scale.

254

20. Note 'IMPORTANT - THE USE OF ADMIRALTY CHARTS'.

243

(a) Reference to the units used for depths measurement. The legend, 'DEPTHS IN FATHOMS/FEET', is shown on certain more recent fathoms charts where confusion might otherwise arise.

241.5
255.2

(b) Conversion scales. To allow approximate conversions between metric and fathoms and feet units. On older charts, conversion tables are given instead.

280

(c) Copyright Notice

B Positions, Distances, Directions, Compass

Geographical Positions

1	Lat	Latitude					
2	Long	Longitude					
3		International Meridian (Greenwich)					
4	°	Degree(s)					130
5	′	Minute(s) of arc					130
6	″	Second(s) of arc					130
7	PA	Position approximate (not accurately determined or does not remain fixed)	†	(PA)	†	(P.A.)	417 424.1
8	PD	Position doubtful (reported in various positions)	†	(PD)	†	(P.D.)	417 424.2
9	N	North					131.1
10	E	East					131.1
11	S	South					131.1
12	W	West					131.1
13	NE	North-east					
14	SE	South-east					
15	NW	North-west					
16	SW	South-west					

Control Points, Distance Marks

20	△	Triangulation point					304.1
21	⊕	Observation spot	†	+ Obs Spot	†	+ Obsn. Spot	304.2
22	⊙ ⊚	Fixed point					305.1 340.5
23	⊼	Benchmark	†	⊼ BM	†	⊼ B.M.	304.3
24		Boundary mark					306
25.1	○ km 32	Distance along waterway, no visible marker					307 361.3
25.2	○ km 32	Distance along waterway, with visible marker					
a		Viewpoint			○ See View		390.2

Symbolised Positions (Examples)

30	⌗ # 18 Wk	Symbols in plan: position is centre of primary symbol					305.1
31	🕯 ⌐ 🔌	Symbols in profile: position is at bottom of symbol					305.1
32	○ Mast ⊙ MAST ★	Point symbols (accurate positions)					305.1 340.5
33	○ Mast PA	Approximate position	†		○ Mast PA		305.1

		Units		
40	km	Kilometre(s)		
41	m	Metre(s)		130
42	dm	Decimetre(s)		130
43	cm	Centimetre(s)		
44	mm	Millimetre(s)		130
45	M	International Nautical Mile(s) (1852m) or Sea Mile(s)	n mile(s) M	130
46		Cable (0.1M)		130
47	ft	Foot/feet		
48		Fathom(s)	fm., fms.	
49	h	Hour		130
50	# m / min	Minute(s) of time		130
51	s / # sec	Second(s) of time	† sec	130
52	kn	Knot(s)		130
53	t	Tonne(s), Ton(s), tonnage (weight)		328.3
54	# cd	Candela		

		Magnetic Compass		
60		Variation	Var	
61		Magnetic	Mag	
62		Bearing		132
63		true		
64		decreasing	decrg	
65		increasing	incrg	
66		Annual change		
67		Deviation		
68.1	# Magnetic Variation 4°30′W 2007 (8′E)	Note of magnetic variation, in position		
68.2	# Magnetic Variation at 55°N 8°W 4°30′W 2007 (8′E)	Note of magnetic variation, out of position	Magnetic Variation: 4°30′W 2007 (10′E)	272.2

B Positions, Distances, Directions, Compass

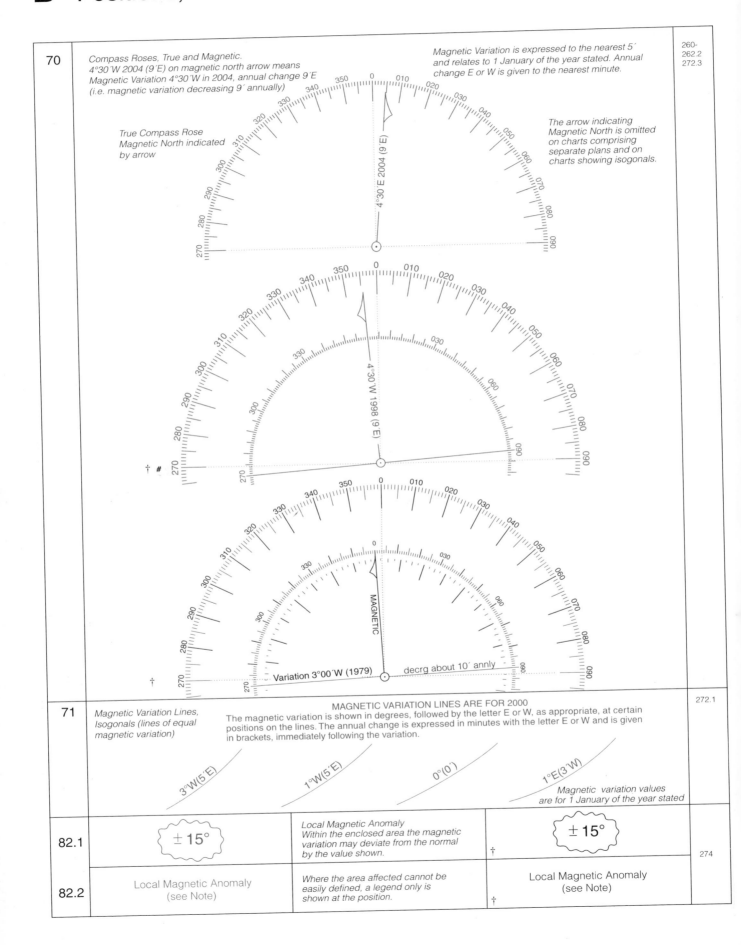

70 Compass Roses, True and Magnetic.
4°30′W 2004 (9′E) on magnetic north arrow means
Magnetic Variation 4°30′W in 2004, annual change 9′E
(i.e. magnetic variation decreasing 9′ annually)

Magnetic Variation is expressed to the nearest 5′
and relates to 1 January of the year stated. Annual
change E or W is given to the nearest minute.

260-
262.2
272.3

True Compass Rose
Magnetic North indicated
by arrow

The arrow indicating
Magnetic North is omitted
on charts comprising
separate plans and on
charts showing isogonals.

4°30′E 2004 (9′E)

4°30′W 1998 (9′E)

† #

MAGNETIC

Variation 3°00′W (1979)   decrg about 10′ annly

†

71 Magnetic Variation Lines,
Isogonals (lines of equal
magnetic variation)

MAGNETIC VARIATION LINES ARE FOR 2000
The magnetic variation is shown in degrees, followed by the letter E or W, as appropriate, at certain
positions on the lines. The annual change is expressed in minutes with the letter E or W and is given
in brackets, immediately following the variation.

272.1

3°W(5′E)   1°W(5′E)   0°(0′)   1°E(3′W)

Magnetic variation values
are for 1 January of the year stated

82.1

± 15°

Local Magnetic Anomaly
Within the enclosed area the magnetic
variation may deviate from the normal
by the value shown.

†

± 15°

274

82.2

Local Magnetic Anomaly
(see Note)

Where the area affected cannot be
easily defined, a legend only is
shown at the position.

†

Local Magnetic Anomaly
(see Note)

8

Foreshore → I, J

Coastline

1		Coastline, surveyed		310.1 310.2
2		Coastline, unsurveyed		311
3		Steep coast, Cliffs रखडी तट ÷ पहरान		312.1
4		Hillocks ठेटा पहडीया		312.1
5		Flat coast		312.2
6		Sandy shore रेनी तट		312.2
7	Stones	Stony shore, Shingly shore कंकड पत्थर से ठका हुआ किनारा		312.2
8	Sand dunes	Sandhills, Dunes बालू का टीला		312.3

2015
10179
36 x 6 = 3£

Plane of Reference for Heights → H

Relief

10	250 200 150 100 50 · 259 200 100	Contour lines with values and spot height		351.3 351.4 351.5 351.6 352.2
11	·437 ·359 ·189 ·115 ·49 ·123	Spot heights		352.1 352.2
12	360 300 ·200 100	Approximate contour lines with values and approximate height		351.3 351.4 351.5 351.6 352.3

C Natural Features

13		Form lines with spot height		351.2 351.3 351.7 352.2
14		Approximate height of top of trees (above height datum)		352.4

Water Features, Lava				
20		River, Stream		353.1 353.2 353.4
21		Intermittent river		353.3
22		Rapids, Waterfalls		353.5
23		Lakes		353.6
24		Salt pans		353.7
25		Glacier		353.8
26		Lava flow		355

			Vegetation	
30		Woods in general		354.1
31		Prominent trees (isolated or in groups)		354.2
31.1		Deciduous tree, unknown or unspecified tree		
31.2		Evergreen (except conifer)		
31.3		Conifer		
31.4		Palm		
31.5		Nipa palm		
31.6		Casuarina		
31.7		Filao		
31.8		Eucalypt		
32		Mangrove		312.4
33		Marsh, Swamp, Salt marsh		312.2

D Cultural Features

Settlements, Buildings

Height of objects → E   Landmarks → E

No.			Description		Ref.
1			Urban area		370.3 370.4
2			Settlement with scattered buildings		370.5
3	○ Name	▭ Name #	Settlement (on medium and small-scale charts)	■ Name	370.7
4	⊹ Name	■ Name HOTEL	Inland village		370.6
5	▬ ■ ▭		Building	Bldg	370.5
6	■ Name Hotel	■ Name Hotel	Important building in built-up area		370.3
7	NAME	NAME	Street name, Road name		371
8	Ru	🕎 Ru	Ruin, Ruined landmark	† 🕎 (ru)	378 378.2

Roads, Railways, Airfields

No.			Description		Ref.
10			Motorway		365.1
11			Road (hard surfaced)		365.2
12			Track, Path (loose or unsurfaced)		365.3
13	# #		Railway, with station	† Rly † Ry † Sta † Stn	328.4 362.1 362.2
14			Cutting	† †	363.2
15			Embankment	† †	364.1
16			Tunnel		363.1
17	Airfield Airport ✈		Airport, Airfield		366.1 366.2
a			Tramway		
b			Helicopter landing site, Heliport	Ⓗ	

Plane of Reference for Heights → H

Other Cultural Features

No.	Symbol		Description	Other Cultural Features		Ref.
20	(20)	(8.9)	Vertical clearance above Height Datum (in parentheses when displaced for clarity)	(17)† / (H 17m)†	(Headway 55ft)†	380.1 380.2
21	⊢23⊣		Horizontal clearance			380.3
22	(20)		Fixed bridge with vertical clearance	(20)†		381.1
23.1	(20)		Opening bridge (in general) with vertical clearance	† (20)		381.3
23.2	7.8 Swing Bridge		Swing bridge with vertical clearance			
23.3	4.2 Lifting Bridge (open 12)		Lifting bridge with vertical clearance (closed and open)			
23.4	12 Bascule Bridge		Bascule bridge with vertical clearance			
23.5	Pontoon Bridge		Pontoon bridge	†		
23.6	5.5 Draw Bridge		Draw bridge with vertical clearance			
24	20 Transporter Bridge		Transporter bridge with vertical clearance between Height Datum and lowest part of structure			381.2
25	20		Overhead transporter, Aerial cableway with vertical clearance	† Transporter (7)		382.3
26	Pyl (28) Pyl		Power transmission line with pylons and safe vertical clearance (see Note below D29)	Power (H 30m) / † Power Overhead (H.98ft)		382.1
27	20		Overhead cable, Telephone line, Telegraph line with vertical clearance	H 20m / † Overhead (H.64ft)		382 382.2
28	20 Overhead pipe		Overhead pipe with vertical clearance			383
29			Pipeline on land	† Pipeline		377

Note: The safe vertical clearance above Height Datum, as defined by the responsible authority, is given in magenta where known (see H20); otherwise the physical vertical clearance is shown in black as in D20.

E Landmarks

General   Plane of Reference for Heights → H   Lighthouses → P   Beacons → Q

No.	Symbol	Description		Ref.
1	⚓ Factory ⊙ Hotel	Examples of landmarks		340.1 340.2 340.5
2	⚓ FACTORY ⊙ HOTEL WATER TOWER	Examples of conspicuous landmarks. A legend in capital letters indicates that a feature is conspicuous	† conspic	340.1 340.2 340.3 340.5
3.1		Pictorial symbols (in true position)		340.7 373.1 390 456.5 457.3
3.2		Sketches, Views (out of position)		
4	(30)	Height of top of a structure above height datum		302.3
5	(30̄)	Height of top of a structure above ground level		303

Landmarks

No.	Symbol	Description		Ref.
10.1	⊹ Ch	Church, Cathedral	† Cath	373.1 373.2
10.2	Tr ⊹ Tr	Church tower		373.2
10.3	Sp ⊹ Sp	Church spire		373.2
10.4	Cup ⊹ Cup	Church cupola		373.2
11		Chapel	⊹ Ch	
12		Cross, Calvary	† #	
13	⋈	Temple	† ⊞	373.3
14	⋈	Pagoda	Pag	373.3
15	⋈	Shinto shrine, Joss house		373.3
16	⋈ 卍 #	Buddhist temple or shrine	† 卍	373.3
17	♀	Mosque, Minaret	† 🕌	373.4
18	⊙ Marabout #	Marabout	⊙ Tomb † ♀	373.5
19	[L L L / L / L L L]	Cemetery (all religions)	† [† † † / † † †] Cemy	373.6

20		Tr	Tower				374.3
21			Water tower, Water tank on a tower	⊙ Water Tr			374.2 376
22		⚫ Chy	Chimney				374.1
23			Flare stack (on land)				374.1
24		Mon	Monument (including column, pillar, obelisk, statue)	† Mont	† Col		374.4
25.1			Windmill				374.5
25.2		⚹ Ru	Windmill (without sails)	† ⚹ (ru)			378.2
26.1			Wind turbine Wind turbine Windmotor	†	† ✿		374.6
26.2			Wind farm				374.6
27	P	FS	Flagstaff, Flagpole				374.7
28			Radio mast, Television mast, Mast	⊙ Radio mast ⊙ TV mast			375.1
29			Radio tower, Television tower	⊙ Radio Tr ⊙ TV Tr			375.2
30.1	⊙ Radar Mast		Radar mast				
30.2	⊙ Radar Tr		Radar tower				487.3
30.3	⊙ Radar Sc		Radar scanner				
30.4	⊙ Radome		Radome				
31			Dish aerial	† ⊙ Dish aerial			375.4
32	• ⊕ ⊕	Tanks	Tanks	† ◯			376.1 376.2
33	◯ Silo	⊙ Silo	Silo				376.3
34.1	Fort		Fortified structure (on large-scale charts)				379.1
34.2			Castle, Fort, Blockhouse (on smaller scale charts)	† ✧ Ft	Cas		379.2
34.3			Battery, Small fort (on smaller scale charts)	† ◡ Batt	Baty		379.2
35.1			Quarry (on large-scale charts)	†			367.1
35.2	⚒		Quarry (on smaller scale charts)				367.2
36	⚒		Mine				367.2

F Ports

Protection Structures							
1			Dyke, Levee, Berm				313.1
2.1			Seawall (on large-scale charts)				313.2
2.2			Seawall (on smaller scale charts)				
3			Causeway				313.3
4.1			Breakwater (in general)				322.1
4.2			Breakwater (loose boulders, tetrapods, etc)		(covers)		
4.3			Breakwater (slope of concrete or masonry)				
5			Training wall				322.2
6.1			Groyne (always dry)				313.4 324
6.2			Groyne (intertidal)				
6.3			Groyne (always underwater)				

Harbour Installations	Depths → I	Anchorages, Limits → N	Beacons and other fixed marks → Q	Marina → U	
10		Fishing harbour			320.1
12		Mole (with berthing facility)			321.3
13		Quay, Wharf		Whf	321.1

No.	Symbol	Description	Alternative	Ref.
14	Pier	Pier, Jetty		321.2 / 321.4
15	Promenade Pier	Promenade pier		321.2
16	Pontoon	Pontoon		326.9
17	Lndg	Landing for boats	† Ldg	324.2
18		Steps, Landing stairs		
19	④ ⑧ (234)	Designation of berth	† ④	323.1
20	○ ▫ ▫ Dn ⦂⦂ Dns	Dolphin		327.1
21	⚏	Deviation dolphin		327.2
22	· ●	Minor post or pile		327.3
23	Slip	Slipway, Patent slip, Ramp		324.1
24		Gridiron, Scrubbing grid		326.8
25		Dry dock, Graving dock	†	326.1
26	Floating Dock	Floating dock	† † †	326.2
27	7·6m	Non-tidal basin, Wet dock		326.3
28		Tidal basin, Tidal harbour		326.4
29.1	Floating Barrier	Floating oil barrier		449.2
29.2		Oil retention barrier (high pressure pipe)		
30	Dock under construction (2004)	Works on land, with year date		329.1
31	Being reclaimed (2004)	Works at sea, Area under reclamation, with year date		329.2
32	Under construction (2004) Works in progress (2004)	Works under construction, with year date	const † constrn. † constn	329 / 329.4

F Ports

33.1		Ru	Ruin		378.1
33.2		⸗⸗⸗ Ru	Ruined pier, partly submerged at high water	⸗⸗⸗ Pier (ru)	
34	Hulk	Hulk	Hulk		
a			Bollard	∘ Bol	

Rivers, Canals, Barrages	*Clearances* → D	*Signal Stations* → T	*Cultural Features* → D	
40			Canal		361.6
41.1	Lock		Lock (on large-scale charts)		326.6 361.6
41.2	≪		Lock (on smaller scale charts)	† ⟵	
42			Caisson, Gate		326.5
43	Flood Barrage		Flood barrage		326.7
44	Dam	E E	Dam, Weir ⟶ Direction of flow		364.2

Transhipment Facilities	*Roads* → D	*Railways* → D	*Tanks* → E	
50	RoRo		Roll-on, Roll-off (RoRo) Ferry Terminal		321.5
51	2 3	2 3	Transit shed, Warehouse (with designation)		328.1
52	♯		Timber yard		328.2
53.1	(3t)		Crane (with lifting capacity) Travelling crane on railway		328.3
53.2	(50t)		Container crane (with lifting capacity)		
53.3	⊙ SHEERLEGS		Sheerlegs (conspicuous)		

Public Buildings				
60	☺	Harbour Master's office	† Hr Mr	325.1
61	⊖	Custom office		325.2
62.1	⊕	Health office, Quarantine building		325.3
62.2	⊕ Hospital	Hospital	⊕ Hosp † Hospl	
63	✉	Post office	† PO	372.1

H Tides, Currents

		Terms Relating to Tidal Levels		
1	CD	Chart Datum *Datum for sounding reduction*		405
2	LAT	*Lowest Astronomical Tide*		405.3
3	HAT	*Highest Astronomical Tide*		
4	MLW	*Mean Low Water*		
5	MHW	*Mean High Water*		
6	MSL	*Mean Sea Level*		
7		*Land survey datum*		
8	MLWS	*Mean Low Water Springs*		
9	MHWS	*Mean High Water Springs*		
10	MLWN	*Mean Low Water Neaps*		
11	MHWN	*Mean High Water Neaps*		
12	MLLW	*Mean Lower Low Water*		
13	MHHW	*Mean Higher High Water*		
14	MHLW	*Mean Higher Low Water*		
15	MLHW	*Mean Lower High Water*		
16	Sp	*Spring tide*	† Spr.	
17	Np	*Neap tide*		
a		*High Water*	HW	
b		*Low Water*	LW	
c		*Mean Tide Level*	MTL	
d		*Ordnance Datum*	OD	

Vertical clearance → D   Tide Gauge → T

Tidal Levels and Charted Data

20

NOTE: Planes of reference are not exactly as shown below for all charts. They are usually defined in notes under chart titles.

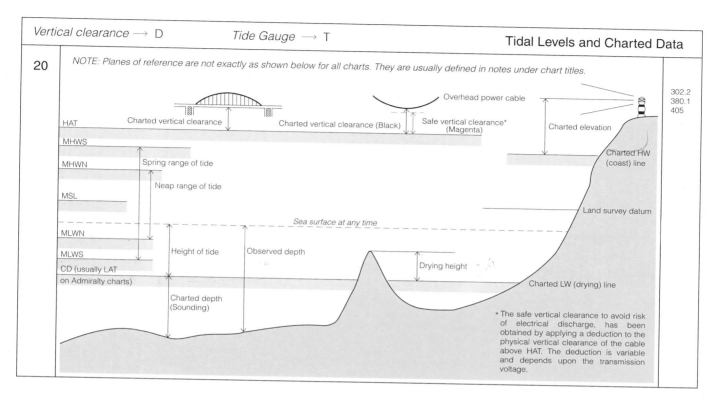

302.2
380.1
405

* The safe vertical clearance to avoid risk of electrical discharge, has been obtained by applying a deduction to the physical vertical clearance of the cable above HAT. The deduction is variable and depends upon the transmission voltage.

Tide Tables

30

Tabular statement of semi-diurnal or diurnal tides

406.2
406.3
406.4
406.5

Tidal Levels referred to Datum of Soundings

Place	Lat. N/S	Long. E/W	Heights in metres/feet above datum				Datum and Remarks
			MHWS	MHWN	MLWN	MLWS	
			MHHW	MLHW	MHLW	MLLW	

31

Tidal stream table

407.2
407.3

Tidal streams referred to....

Hours	◇ Geographical Position	Directions of streams (degrees)	Rates at spring tides (knots)	Rates at neap tides (knots)	Ⓐ	Ⓑ	Ⓒ	Ⓓ	Ⓔ
Before High Water 6					-6				
5					-5				No
4					-4				
3					-3				Maximum Rates
2					-2				
1					-1				
High Water					0				For predictions, use Admiralty Tide Tables
After High Water 1					+1				
2					+2				
3					+3				
4					+4				
5					+5				
6					+6				

H Tides, Currents

Tidal Streams and Currents			Breakers ⟶ K	Tide Gauge ⟶ T	
40	_3kn_ →	Flood tide stream (with mean spring rate)	† → • • →	The number of black dots on the tidal stream arrows indicates the number of hours after High or Low Water at which the streams are running	407.4 408.2
41	_2, 8kn_ →	Ebb tide stream (with mean spring rate)	† → • • • →		407.4 408.2
42	# »»» → ∿∿∿ →	Current in restricted waters	† »»» →		408.2
43	∿∿∿ → (see Note)	Ocean current. Details of current strength and seasonal variations may be shown			408.3
44	≋ ≋ ≋ ≋	Overfalls, tide rips, races	† ≋		423.1
45	◎ ◎ ◎ ◎ ◎ ◎ ◎	Eddies			423.3
46	◇Ď◇	Position of tabulated tidal stream data with designation	† ◇Ď◇		407.2
47	[a]	Offshore position for which tidal levels are tabulated			406.5
e		Wave recorder		◦ _Wave recorder_	
f		Current meter		◦ _Current meter_	

22

							General
1	*ED*		Existence doubtful	†		*(ED)*	417 424.3
2	:40: *SD*		Sounding of doubtful depth				417 424.4
3.1	*Rep*		Reported, but not confirmed	†		*Repd*	417 424.5
3.2	*Rep (1973)*		Reported, with year of report, but not confirmed	†		*Repd (1973)*	
4	:184:	:212:	Reported, but not confirmed, sounding or danger (on small-scale charts only)				M-4 Part C 404.3
a			Unexamined			*unexam* †*unexamd*	

<table>
<tr><td colspan="2">Plane of Reference for Depths → H</td><td>Plane of Reference for Heights → H</td><td colspan="3">Soundings and Drying Heights</td></tr>
<tr><td>10</td><td>12   9₂   # ^{9,7}</td><td>Sounding in true position</td><td colspan="3"></td><td>403.1 410/412 412.1</td></tr>
</table>

10	12 9_2 # $9,7$		Sounding in true position				403.1 410/412 412.1
11	•(4_8) + (12) 3349		Sounding out of position	•(8_3) (10_4)	+ 1_8 8_7 7_1		412 412.1 412.2
12	(14_7)		Least depth in narrow channel				412 412.1 412.2
13	$\overline{330}$		No bottom found at depth shown				412.3
14	12 9_1		Soundings taken from old or smaller scale sources shown in upright, hairline figures				412.4 417.3
15	4_9 4 0_9 3_4 2 0		Drying heights and contours above chart datum				413 413.1 413.2
16	1_4 0 0_6 2_5 1_7 2_7		Natural watercourse (in intertidal area)				413.3

<table>
<tr><td colspan="2">Plane of Reference for Depths → H</td><td colspan="2">Depths in Fairways and Areas</td></tr>
</table>

20	– – – – – – – – – –	Limit of dredged channel or area (major and minor)	# _____	414.3
21	7·0m 3·5m	Dredged channel or area with depth of dredging in metres and decimetres	Depths may be shown as $3,5$ or 3_5 on some adopted charts	414
22	17m (2006) Dredged to 8·2m (2006)	Dredged channel or area with depth of dredging and year of the latest control survey		414.1
23	17·0m Maintained depth 13·5m	Dredged channel or area with depth regularly maintained		414.2

Depths

24		Area swept by wire drag. The depth is shown at Chart Datum. (The latest date of sweeping may be shown in parentheses)		415 415.1
25		Unsurveyed or inadequately surveyed area; area with inadequate depth information		410 417 417.6 417.7

Depth Contours

30		Drying contour Low Water (LW) Line, Chart Datum (CD) Blue tint, in one or more shades, and tint ribbons, are shown to different limits according to the scale and purpose of the chart and the nature of the bathymetry. On some charts, the standard set of contours is augmented by additional contours in order to delimit particular bathymetric features or for the benefit of particular categories of shipping. However, in some instances where the provision of additional contours would be helpful, the survey data available does not permit it. On some charts, contours and labels are printed in blue.	On charts showing depths in fathoms/feet, the following contours are used: On some recently-corrected charts, contours may be shown by continuous lines.	404.2 410 411
31		Approximate depth contours (length of dashes may vary)		411.2 417.5

Rocks → K				Types of Seabed	
1	*S*	*Sand*	†	s	425 427
2	*M*	*Mud*	†	m	
3	*Cy*	*Clay*	†	cl	
4	*Si*	*Silt*			
5	*St*	*Stones*	†	st	
6	*G*	*Gravel*	†	g	
7	*P*	*Pebbles*	†	peb	
8	*Cb*	*Cobbles*			
9.1	*R*	*Rock, Rocky*	†	r	
9.2	*Bo*	*Boulder(s)*			421.2
10	*Co*	*Coral*	†	crl	
11	*Sh*	*Shells*	†	sh	
12.1	*S/M*	*Two layers e.g. Sand over Mud*	#M (25)/SG S (<1)/R (Thickness of surface layer in metres)		425.8
12.2	*fS.M.Sh*	*Mixed: where the seabed comprises a mixture of materials, the main constituent is given first, e.g. fine Sand with Mud and Shells*			425.9
13.1	*Wd*	*Weed (including Kelp)*	†	wd	425.5
13.2		*Kelp*			428.2
14		*Sandwaves*			428.1
15		*Spring in seabed*			428.3
a		*Ground*	†	*Gd* grd	
b		*Ooze*	†	*Oz*	
c		*Marl*	†	*Ml*	
d		*Shingle*	†	*Sn* shin	
e		*Chalk*	†	*Ck* chk	
f		*Quartz*	†	*Qz* qrtz	
g		*Madrepore*	†	*Md* mad	
h		*Basalt*	†	*Ba*	
i		*Lava*	†	*Lv*	
j		*Pumice*	†	*Pm* pum	
k		*Tufa*	†	*T*	
l		*Scoriæ*	†	*Sc*	
m		*Cinders*	†	*Cn* cin	

J   Nature of the Seabed

n		Manganese	†	Mn	man	
o		Glauconite	†	Gc		
p		Oysters	†	Oy	oys	
q		Mussels	†	Ms	mus	
r		Sponge	†	Sp		
s		Algae	†	Al		
t		Foraminifera	†	Fr	for	
u		Globigerina	†	Gl		
v		Diatoms	†	Di		
w		Radiolaria	†	Rd	rad	
x		Pteropods	†	Pt		
y		Polyzoa	†	Po	pol	

Intertidal Areas

20		Area of sand and mud with patches of stones or gravel			426.1
21		Rocky area			426.2
22		Coral reef			426.3

Qualifying Terms

30	f	Fine				425 427
31	m	Medium	only used in relation to sand			
32	c	Coarse				
33	bk	Broken	†		brk	
34	sy	Sticky	†		stk	
35	so	Soft	†		sft	
36	sf	Stiff	†		stf	
37	v	Volcanic	†		vol	
38	ca	Calcareous	†		cal	
39	h	Hard				425.5 425.7

aa		Small	†		sm	
ab		Large	†		l	
ac		Glacial	†	ga	glac	
ad		Speckled	†	sk	spk	
ae		White	†		w	
af		Black	†	bl	blk	
ag		Blue	†		b	
ah		Green	†		gn	
ai		Yellow	†		y	
aj		Red	†		rd	
ak		Brown	†		br	
al		Chocolate	†	ch	choc	
am		Grey	†		gy	
an		Light	†		lt	
ao		Dark	†		d	

K Rocks, Wrecks, Obstructions

General

1		*Dangerline: A danger line draws attention to a danger which would not stand out clearly enough if represented solely by its symbol (e.g. isolated rock) or delimits an area containing numerous dangers, through which it is unsafe to navigate*			411.4 420.1
2	7_5	*Depth cleared by wire drag sweep or diver. The symbol may be used with other symbols, e.g. wrecks, obstructions, wells*			415 422.3 422.9
3	*(12)*	*Safe clearance depth. Obstruction over which the exact depth is unknown, but which is considered to have a safe clearance at the depth shown. The symbol may be used with other symbols, e.g. wrecks, wells, turbines*			422.5 422.7
a		*Dries*	† *Dr*	† *dr*	
b		*Covers*	† *cov*		
c		*Uncovers*	† *uncov*		

Rocks

			Plane of Reference for Heights → H	*Plane of Reference for Depths* → H	
10		*Rock (islet) which does not cover, height above height datum*	(1,7) (3,1) (4,1)		421.1
11		*Rock which covers and uncovers, height above Chart Datum, where known*	† *Dries 1·6m* † *Dr 1·6m*		421.2
12		*Rock awash at the level of Chart Datum*			421.3
13		*Underwater rock over which the depth is unknown, but which is considered dangerous to surface navigation*			421.4
14		*Underwater rock of known depth:*			421.4
14.1		*inside the corresponding depth area*			
14.2		*outside the corresponding depth area, dangerous to surface navigation*			

15	35 R	Underwater rock of known depth, not dangerous to surface navigation			421.4
16	+ Co + + Co + 5_8	Coral reef which is always covered			421.5
17	⌣⌣ 5_8 Br 19 18	Breakers			423.2
d		Discoloured water	Discol	† Discold	424.6

	Hulk → F	Plane of Reference for Depths → H	Historic Wreck → N **Wrecks and Fouls**		
20		Wreck, hull never covers, on large-scale charts			422.1
21		Wreck, hull covers and uncovers, on large-scale charts	† Wk	† Wk	422.1
22	5_5 Wk 6_5 Wk	Submerged wreck, depth known, on large-scale charts	† 5_2 Wk		422.1
23	Wk	Submerged wreck, depth unknown, on large-scale charts	† Wk		422.1
24		Wreck showing any part of hull or superstructure at the level of Chart Datum			422.2
25	Masts	Wreck of which the mast(s) only are visible at Chart Datum	Mast (1·2) Wk Funnel Mast ($\underline{1}_2$)		422.2
26	4_6 Wk 25 Wk	Wreck over which the depth has been obtained by sounding but not by wire sweep			422.4
27	4_6 Wk 25 Wk	Wreck, least depth obtained by wire sweep or diver			422.3
28		Wreck, depth unknown, which is considered potentially dangerous to surface navigation			422.5
29	⧾⧾⧾	Wreck, in over 200m or depth unknown, which is considered not dangerous to surface navigation. For information about depth criteria, which may vary, see NP100, The Mariner's Handbook			422.6
e		Submerged wreck, depth unknown	† Wk		

30	20 Wk	Wreck over which the exact depth is unknown, but which is considered to have a safe clearance at the depth shown		422.5 422.7
31	_F o u l_ #	Foul area, not dangerous to surface navigation, but to be avoided by vessels anchoring, trawling, etc (eg remains of wreck, cleared platform)	† Foul † Foul 22 Foul _(where depth known)_	422.8
f		Navigation light on stranded wreck		

Obstructions		Plane of Reference for Depths → H Kelp, Seaweed → J Underwater Installations → L		
40	_Obstn_ Obstn	Obstruction or danger to navigation the exact nature of which is not specified or has not been determined, depth unknown		422.9
41	4₆ Obstn 16₈ Obstn	Obstruction, depth obtained by sounding but not wire sweep		422.9
42	4₆ Obstn 16₈ Obstn	Obstruction, least depth obtained by wire sweep or diver		422.9
43.1	Obstn ⊤ ⊤ ⊤ #	Stumps of posts or piles, wholly submerged		327.5
43.2	⊤ #	Submerged pile, stake, snag or stump (with exact position)		
44.1		Fishing stakes	† ╧ ╪ ╪ ╧ †	447.1
44.2		Fish trap, fish weir, tunny nets	†	447.2
45	_Fish traps_ _Tunny nets_	Fish trap area, tunny nets area	——— —— —— ——— _(U.S. waters only)_	447.3
46.1	🐟 🐟	Fish haven		447.5
46.2	🐟 2₄ 🐟 (2₄)	Fish haven, with minimum depth		
47	_Shellfish Beds_	Shellfish beds, with no obstruction to navigation		447.4
48.1		Marine farm (on large-scale charts)	† _Fish farm_ † _Fish cages_	447.6
48.2		Marine farm (on small-scale charts)		

Combined symbols → K *(General)*		*Areas, Limits* → N			General
1	*EKOFISK* *OILFIELD*	Name of oilfield or gasfield			445.3
2	⊡ Z-44	Platform with designation/name	† ★	† ⊡	445.3
3		Limit of safety zone around offshore installation			439.2 445.16
4		Limit of development area			
5.1	⊥ ⊥ Fl.Y ⊥ 18	Wind turbine, lit wind turbine and wind turbine with vertical clearance			445.8
5.2		Wind farm, wind farm with restricted area			445.9

Mooring Buoys → Q					Platforms and Moorings
10		Production platform, Platform, Oil derrick	† ★	† ⊡	445.2
11	⊡ Fla	Flare stack (at sea)			445.2
12	⊡ SPM	Fixed Single Point Mooring, including Single Anchor Leg Mooring (SALM), Articulated Loading Column (ALC)			445.2 445.4
13		Observation / research platform (with name)		⊡ Name	
14		Disused platform		⊡ (disused)	
15		Artificial Island		Name	
16		Floating Single Point Mooring, including Catenary Anchor Leg Mooring (CALM), Single Buoy Mooring (SBM)			445.4
17		Moored storage tanker including FSU and FPSO			445.5
18	⊶→	Mooring ground tackle for fixing floating structures			431.6

Plane of Reference for Depths → H		*Obstructions* → K			Underwater Installations
20	⟨15⟩ Prod Well ◯ Prod Well	Production well, with depth where known		◌ Well	445.5
21.1	◌ Well	Suspended well (wellhead and pipes projecting from the seabed) over which the depth is unknown			445.1
21.2	⟨15⟩ Well	Suspended well over which the depth is known			445.1
21.3	◌ Well (5.7) #	Suspended well with height of wellhead above the sea floor			
22	#	Site of cleared platform			422.8

L Offshore Installations

23	⬦ ⊙ Pipe ◉ Pipe (1₈)	Above-water wellhead (lit and unlit). The drying height or height above height datum is charted if known		445.1
24	⬦ Turbine ◤ FL(2) ☆ Underwater Turbine	Underwater turbine		445.10
c		Single Well Oil Production System. The depth shown is the least depth over the wellhead. For substantial periods of time a loading tanker is positioned over the wellhead	⬦ 93 SWOPS	445.1
d		Underwater installations; template, manifold	⬦ Template ⬦ Manifold	445.1

Submarine Cables

30.1	∿∿∿∿∿	Submarine cable	† ∿∿∿∿∿	443.1
30.2	⊤⊤⊤⊤ ∿∿∿ ⊤⊤⊤ ⊥⊥⊥⊥ ∿∿∿ ⊥⊥⊥⊥	Submarine cable area	† ----- Cable Area -----	443.2 439.3
31.1	∿∿∿ ⌇ ∿∿∿	Submarine power cable	† ∿∿ Power ∿∿ † ∿∿ Power ∿∿	443.2
31.2	⊤⊤⊤⊤ ∿∿⌇∿∿ ⊤⊤⊤ ⊥⊥⊥⊥ ∿∿⌇∿∿ ⊥⊥⊥⊥	Submarine power cable area	† ----- Power Cable Area -----	443.2 439.3
32	∿∿∿∿	Disused submarine cable		443.7

Submarine Pipelines

40.1	→→→→ Oil →→→→ Gas →→→→ Chem →→→→ Water →→→→	Supply pipeline: unspecified, oil, gas, chemicals, water	† --- Pipeline ---	444 444.1
40.2	→→⊤⊤⊤⊤→→ ←←⊥⊥⊥⊥←← →→⊤⊤⊤ Oil ⊤⊤⊤→→ Gas ←←⊥⊥⊥ ⊥⊥⊥←← →→⊤⊤⊤ Chem ⊤⊤⊤→→ Water ←←⊥⊥⊥ ⊥⊥⊥←←	Supply pipeline area: unspecified, oil, gas, chemicals, water	† ⌐ Pipeline Area ⌐ † ⌐ Pipeline Area ⌐	444.3 439.3
41.1	→→→ Water →→ Sewer →→ Outfall →→ Intake →→	Outfall and intake: unspecified, water, sewer, outfall, intake	† --- Sewer --- † --- Outfall ---	444 444.2
41.2	→→⊤⊤⊤⊤→→ ←←⊥⊥⊥⊥←← →→⊤⊤⊤ Water ⊤⊤⊤→→ Sewer ←←⊥⊥⊥ ⊥⊥⊥←← →→⊤⊤⊤ Outfall ⊤⊤⊤→→ Intake ←←⊥⊥⊥ ⊥⊥⊥←←	Outfall and intake area: unspecified, water, sewer, outfall, intake	† ⌐ Pipeline Area ⌐ † ⌐ Pipeline Area ⌐	444.3 439.3
42	→→ Buried 1·6m →→	Buried pipeline / pipe (with nominal depth to which buried)		444.5
43	→→→→→ ⬦ 3₂ Obstn	Diffuser, crib	→→→→→ ⬦ 3₂ Diffuser	444.8
44	→→ →→ →→ →→ → → → → →→ →→ →→ → → →	Disused pipeline / pipe		444.7

Tracks Marked by Lights → P		*Leading Beacons* → Q			Tracks
1	270·5° 2 Bns ≠ 270·5°	Leading line (≠ means "in line", the continuous line is the track to be followed)	Bn Bn *Bns in Line 270°30'* *Ldg Bns 270·5°* *270·5°*	433.1 433.2 433.3
2	270·5° Island open of Headland 270·5°	Transit (other than leading line), Clearing line	Bns in line 270·5°	433.4 433.5
3	090°-270°	Recommended track based on a system of fixed marks	† → † ← → †	434.1 434.2
4	090°-270°	Recommended track not based on a system of fixed marks	— — < — —DW— — —270°— — — — — < — —	434.1 434.2
5.1	DW (see Note)	One-way track and DW track based on a system of fixed marks	† ← † - - - - - - ← - - - - - -	
5.2	270° DW	One-way track and DW track not based on a system of fixed marks		432.3
6	<7·3m> - - - - <7·3m> - - - - -	Recommended track with maximum authorised draught		432.4 434.3 434.4

				Routeing Measures - Basic Symbols	
10	⇒	Established (mandatory) direction of traffic flow		435.1
11	⇢	Recommended direction of traffic flow		435.5
12		Separation line (large-scale, small-scale)		435.1 436.3
13		Separation zone		435.1 436.3
14		Limit of restricted routeing measure (e.g. Inshore Traffic Zone, Area to be Avoided)		435.1 436.3 439.2
15		Limit of routeing measure		435.1 436.3
16	⚠ Precautionary Area	Precautionary area		435.2
17	ASL (see Note)	Archipelagic Sea Lane; axis line and limit beyond which vessels shall not navigate	ASL (see Note)	435.10
18	FAIRWAY 7.3m FAIRWAY <7.3m>	Fairway, designated by regulatory authority: with minimum depth with maximum authorised draught		

‡ The term 'recommended' in connection with tracks and routeing measures does not imply recommendation by the United Kingdom Hydrographic Office. It is usually by a regulatory authority, but may be established by precedent.

M Tracks, Routes

Examples of Routeing Measures

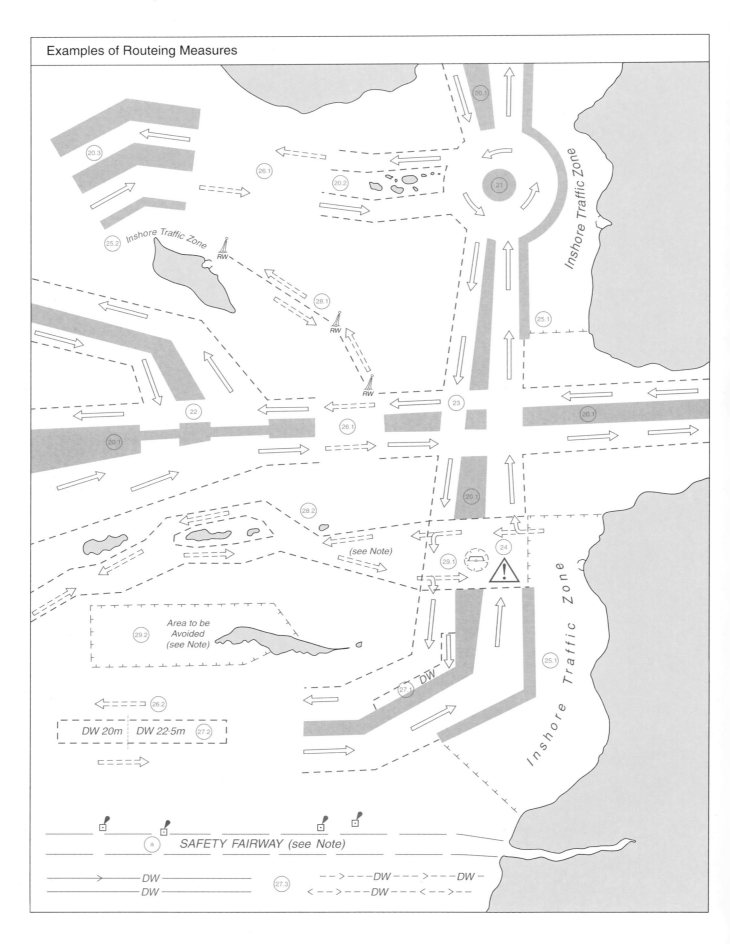

Examples of Routeing Measures (see diagram on page 34)

(20.1)	Traffic separation scheme (TSS), traffic separated by separation zone	435.1
(20.2)	Traffic separation scheme, traffic separated by natural obstructions	435.1
(20.3)	Traffic separation scheme, with outer separation zone, separating traffic using scheme from traffic not using it	435.1
(21)	Traffic separation scheme, roundabout	435.1
(22)	Traffic separation scheme with "crossing gates"	435.1
(23)	Traffic separation schemes crossing, without designated precautionary area	435.1
(24)	Precautionary area	435.2
(25.1)	Inshore traffic zone (ITZ), with defined end limits	435.1
(25.2)	Inshore traffic zone, without defined end limits	435.1
‡ (26.1)	Recommended direction of traffic flow, between traffic separation schemes	435.5
‡ (26.2)	Recommended direction of traffic flow, for ships not needing a deep water route	435.5
(27.1)	Deep water route (DW), as part of one-way traffic lane	435.3
(27.2)	Two-way deep water route, with minimum depth stated	435.3
(27.3)	Deep water route, centre line shown as recommended one-way or two-way track	435.3
‡ (28.1)	Recommended route (often marked by centre line buoys)	435.4
(28.2)	Two-way route with one-way sections	435.6
(29.1)	Area to be avoided (ATBA), around navigational aid	435.7
(29.2)	Area to be avoided, because of danger of stranding	435.7
(a)	Safety fairway	432.2

‡ The term 'recommended' in connection with tracks and routeing measures does not imply recommendation by the United Kingdom Hydrographic Office. It is usually by a regulatory authority, but may be established by precedent.

Radar Surveillance System

30	Radar Surveillance Station	Radar surveillance station		487 487.3
31	Ra Cuxhaven	Radar range		487.1
32.1	——— Ra ———	Radar reference line		487.2
32.2	Ra 090° - 270°	Radar reference line coinciding with a leading line		

Radio Reporting

40.1		Radio calling-in point, way point, or reporting point (with designation, if any) showing direction(s) of vessel movement	‡	488
40.2		Radio reporting line (with designation, if any) showing direction(s) of vessel movement	‡	488.1

Ferries

50		Ferry	‡ Ferry / ‡ Ferry	438.1
51	Cable Ferry	Cable Ferry		438.2

N Areas, Limits

General	Dredged and Swept Areas → I	Submarine Cables, Submarine Pipelines → L	Tracks Routes → M	

1.1	*(for emphasis)*	Maritime limit in general, usually implying permanent physical obstructions		439.1 439.6
1.2	*(for emphasis)*	Maritime limit in general, usually implying no permanent physical obstructions		
2.1	*(for emphasis)*	Limit of restricted area		439.2 439.3 439.6 441.6
2.2		Limit of area into which entry is prohibited	† Entry Prohibited	

Anchorages, Anchorage Areas

10	⚓	Reported anchorage (no defined limits)	† ⚓	431.1
11.1	Ⓐ N53 ⑭	Anchor berths	† N53	431.2
11.2	(Ⓐ) (N53) (⑭)	Anchor berths with swinging circle shown	† (N53)	
12.1	⚓ ⚓	Anchorage area in general		431.3
12.2	⚓ No 1 ⚓ ⚓	Numbered anchorage area	† ① † ①	
12.3	⚓ Oaze ⚓ ⚓	Named anchorage area		
12.4	⚓ DW ⚓ ⚓	Deep water anchorage area, anchorage area for deep-draught vessels		
12.5	⚓ Tanker ⚓ ⚓	Tanker anchorage area. This symbol may be adapted for other types of vessel, e.g. small craft		
12.6	⚓ 24h ⚓ ⚓	Anchorage area for periods up to 24 hours		
12.7	⚓ ⚓ ⚓	Explosives anchorage area		
12.8	⚓ ⊕ ⚓ ⚓	Quarantine anchorage area		
12.9	⚓ Reserved (see Note) ⚓ ⚓	Reserved anchorage area		
13		Seaplane operating area	†	449.6
14	⚓	Anchorage for seaplanes	† ⚓	449.6

				Restricted Areas
20		Anchoring prohibited	Anchoring Prohibited	431.4 439.3 439.4
21		Fishing prohibited		439.3 439.4
22	*Example* ⊤⊤ MR ⊤⊤⊤ MR ⊤⊤⊤	Environmentally Sensitive Sea Areas: Limit of marine reserve, national park, non-specific nature reserve	Marine Nature Reserve (see Note)	437.3 437.6 437.7
	Examples	Bird sanctuary, seal sanctuary (other animal silhouettes may be used for specialized areas)		
	PSSA	Particularly Sensitive Sea Area (coloured tint band may vary in width between 1 and 5mm)		
23.1	Explosives Dumping Ground	Explosives dumping ground	Explosives Dumping Ground	442.1 442.2 442.3 442.4
23.2	Explosives Dumping Ground (disused)	Explosives dumping ground (disused)	Explosives Dumping Ground (disused)	
24	Dumping Ground for Chemicals	Dumping ground for chemical waste		442.1 442.2 442.3
25	Degaussing Range	Degaussing range	† D.G. Range DG Range	448.1 448.2
26	Historic Wk	Historic wreck and restricted area		449.5
27	5kn	Maximum speed		430.2
a		Seabed operations dangerous/prohibited		
b		Diving prohibited		
				Military Practice Areas
30		Firing practice area		441.1 441.2 441.3
31		Military restricted area into which entry is prohibited	Entry Prohibited	441.6
32		Mine-laying (and counter-measure) practice area		441.4
33	SUBMARINE EXERCISE AREA	Submarine transit lane and exercise area		441.5
34	Minefield	Minefield	Mine Danger Area (see Note)	441.8

N Areas, Limits

International Boundaries and National Limits

40	DANMARK +++++++++++++++++++++ DEUTSCHLAND	International boundary on land	† DENMARK +++++++++++++++++++++ GERMANY ·—·—·—·—·—·—	440.1
41	UNITED KINGDOM —·—+—·—+—·—+—·—+— NORGE	International maritime boundary	† UNITED KINGDOM —·—+—·—+—·—+—·—+— NORWAY ·—·—·—·—·—·— † Continental Shelf — — — — Boundary — — — —	440.3
42	Straight territorial sea baseline with base point			440.4
43	——————— ++ ———————	Seaward limit of Territorial Sea	# +++++++++++++++++++++++	440.5
44	——————— + ———————	Seaward limit of Contiguous Zone		440.6
45	—·⊂▷·— —·⊂▷·— —·⊂▷·— —·⊂▷·—	National fishery limits		440.7
46	——— Continental Shelf ———	Limit of Continental Shelf		440.8
47	——— EEZ ———	Limit of Exclusive Economic Zone	# ——— ++ ——— ++ ———	440.9
48	— —⊖— — — — —⊖— —	Customs limit		440.2
49	Harbour Limit	Harbour limit	† Harbour Limit	430.1

Various Limits

60.1	(2008) / ꟷꟷꟷꟷ # / ꟳꟳꟳ	Limit of fast ice, Ice front (with date)		449.1
60.2	(2008) / ꟷꟷꟷꟷ # / ꟳꟳꟳ	Limit of sea ice (pack ice) seasonal (with date)	†	
61	Log Pond	Floating barrier, including log ponds, security barriers, ice booms, shark nets	† Booming Ground † Timber	449.2
62.1	Spoil Ground	Spoil ground		446.1 446.2
62.2	Spoil Ground (disused)	Spoil ground (disused)		
63	Extraction Area	Extraction (dredging) area	† Dredging Area	446.4
64	Cargo Transhipment Area	Cargo transhipment area		449.4
65	† Incineration Area	Incineration area	† Area for burning refuse material	449.3

Beacons → Q				**Light Structures, Major Floating Lights**	
1	⭐ ⭐ Lt LtHo		Major light, minor light ‡, light, lighthouse	# !	470.5
2			Lighted offshore platform		445.2
3	⭐ BnTr BY		Lighted beacon tower ‡	† Bn Tower † Bn Tr	456.4 457.1 457.2
4	⭐ R BRB ⭐ Bn		Lighted beacon ‡ On smaller scale charts, where navigation within recognition range of the daymark is unlikely, lighted beacons are charted solely as lights	R BRB G R #	457.1 457.2
5	R ⭐ Bn		Lighted buoyant beacon, resilient beacon ‡		459.1 459.2
6			Major floating light (light vessel, major light float, Large Automatic Navigational Buoy (LANBY))	† LtV	462.9 474
a			Navigation lights on landmarks or other structures		

‡ *Minor lights, fixed and floating, usually conform to IALA Maritime Buoyage System characteristics*

	Bearings of Light Off Chart Limits
b	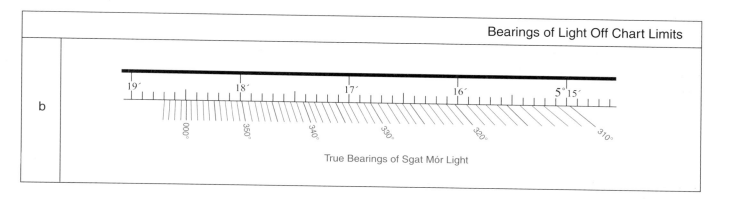

True Bearings of Sgat Mór Light

P Lights

	Light Characters			*Light Characters on Light Buoys* → Q	
	Abbreviation		*Class of Light*	*Illustration*	*Period shown* ⊢
	International	*National*			
10.1	F		Fixed		
10.2	*Occulting (total duration of light longer than total duration of darkness)*				
	Oc	† Occ	Single-occulting		
	Oc(2) *Example*	† GpOcc(2) *Example*	Group-occulting		
	Oc(2+3) *Example*	† GpOcc(2+3) *Example*	Composite group-occulting		
10.3	*Isophase (duration of light and darkness equal)*				
	Iso		Isophase		
10.4	*Flashing (total duration of light shorter than total duration of darkness)*				
	Fl		Single-flashing		
	Fl(3) *Example*	† GpFl(3) *Example*	Group-flashing		
	Fl(2+1) *Example*	† GpFl(2+1) *Example*	Composite group-flashing		
10.5	LFl		Long-flashing (flash 2s or longer)		
10.6	*Quick (repetition rate of 50 to 79 - usually either 50 or 60 - flashes per minute)*				
	Q	† QkFl	Continuous quick		
	Q(3) *Example*	† QkFl(3) *Example*	Group quick		
	IQ	† IntQkFl	Interrupted quick		
10.7	*Very quick (repetition rate of 80 to 159 - usually either 100 or 120 - flashes per minute)*				
	VQ	† VQkFl	Continuous very quick		
	VQ(3) *Example*	† VQkFl(3) *Example*	Group very quick		
	IVQ	† IntVQkFl	Interrupted very quick		
10.8	*Ultra quick (repetition rate of 160 or more - usually 240 to 300 - flashes per minute)*				
	UQ		Continuous ultra quick		
	IUQ		Interrupted ultra quick		
10.9	Mo(K) *Example*		Morse Code		
10.10	FFl		Fixed and flashing		
10.11	Al.WR *Example*	† Alt.WR *Example*	Alternating		

40

Lights P

Colours of Lights and Marks

11.1	W		White (for lights, only on sector and alternating lights)			450.2 450.3 470.4 470.6 471.4 475.1
11.2	R		Red			
11.3	G		Green			
11.4	Bu		Blue	†	Bl	
11.5	Vi		Violet			
11.6	Y		Yellow			
11.7	Y	# Or	Orange	†	Or	
11.8	Y	# Am	Amber			

| | | | Colours of lights shown on:
standard charts
on multicoloured charts
on multicoloured charts at sector lights | | | |

Period

12	90s 2·5s *Examples*	Period in seconds and tenths of a second	†	90sec	471.5

Plane of Reference for Heights → H   Tidal Levels → H

Elevation

13	12m *Example*	Elevation of light given in metres	*On fathoms charts, the elevation of a light is given in feet e.g.* **40ft**	471.6

Range

Note: Charted ranges are nominal ranges given in sea miles

14	15M *Example*	Light with single range			471.7 471.9 475.5
	15/10M *Example*	Light with two different ranges	†	15,10M	
	15-7M *Example*	Light with three or more ranges	†	15,10,7M	

Disposition

15	(hor)	horizontally disposed	†	(horl.)	471.8
	(vert)	vertically disposed	†	(vertl.)	471.8

Example of a full Light Description 471.9

16	**Example** *of a light description on a* **metric** *chart using international abbreviations:* ★ Fl(3)WRG.15s13m7-5M		**Example** *of a light description on a* **fathoms** *chart using international abbreviations:* ★ Al.Fl.WR.30s110ft23/22M
	Fl(3)	**Class** or **character** of light: in this example a group-flashing light, regularly repeating a group of three flashes.	Al.Fl.	**Class** or **character** of light: in this example exhibiting single flashes of differing colours alternately.
	WRG.	**Colours** of light: white, red and green, exhibiting the different colours in defined sectors.	WR.	**Colours** of light shown alternately: white and red all-round (ie, not a sector light).
	15s	**Period** of light in seconds, i.e., the time taken to exhibit one full sequence of 3 flashes and eclipses: 15 seconds.	30s	**Period** of light in seconds, ie, the time taken to exhibit the sequence of two flashes and two eclipses: 30 seconds.
	13m	**Elevation** of focal plane above height datum: 13 metres.	110ft	**Elevation** of focal plane above height datum: 110 feet.
	7-5M	**Luminous range** in sea miles: the distance at which a light of a particular intensity can be seen in 'clear' visibilty, taking no account of earth curvature. In those countries (eg United Kingdom) where the term 'clear' is defined as a meteorological visibilty of 10 sea miles, the range may be termed "**nominal**". In this example the ranges of the colours are: white 7 miles, green 5 miles, red between 7 and 5 miles.	23/22M	**Range** in sea miles. Until 1971 the lesser of **geographical** range (based on a height of eye of 15 feet) and **luminous** range was charted. Now, when the charts are corrected, luminous (or nominal) range is given. In this example the luminous ranges of the colours are: white 23 miles, red 22 miles. The geographical range can be found from the table in the Admiralty List of Lights (for the elevation of 110 feet, it would be 16 miles).

P Lights

Lights marking Fairways	Note: Quoted bearings are always from seaward

Leading Lights and Lights in line

20.1	Oc.225·3° Oc.6s Oc.3s Oc.3s8m12M ★ ★ Oc.6s24m15M	Leading lights with leading line (the firm line is the track to be followed) and arcs of visibility	Ldg Lts 225·3° Oc.6s Oc.3s Oc.3s8m12M ★ † ★ Oc.6s24m15M	433 433.1 433.2 433.3 475.1 475.6
20.2	Oc.4s12M ★ ★ Oc.R. 4s10M Oc&Oc.R ≠ 269·3°	Leading lights (≠ means "in line"; the firm line is the track to be followed; the light descriptions will be at the light stars or on the leading line, not usually both).	Occ.4s12M ★ ★ Occ.R. 4s10M † Lights in line 269°18′	433.2 433.3 475.6
20.3	LdgOc.W&R ★●━	Leading lights on small-scale charts	Oc.W&R ★●╌╌ 265°	433.1 475.6
21	Fl.G Fl.G ★ ★ 270° 2Fl.R ★● 270°	Lights in line (marking the sides of a channel)	Lights in line 092° † ★ ★ Fl Fl	433.4 475.6
22	Rear Lt or Upper Lt	Rear or upper light	Upr. †	470.7
23	Front Lt or Lower Lt	Front or lower light	Lr †	470.7

Direction Lights

30.1	★● Dir 269° Fl(2)5s10m11M	Direction light with narrow sector and course to be followed, flanked by darkness or unintensified light	DirLt †	
30.2	Oc.12s6M ★ Dir 299° Dir 255·5° ★● Fl(2)15s11M	Direction light with course to be followed, uncharted sector is flanked by darkness or unintensified light	DirLt †	471.3 471.9 475 475.1 475.5 475.7
30.3	F.G Al.WG Oc.W.4s F.R Al.WR ★● DirWRG. 15-5M	Direction light with narrow fairway sector flanked by light sectors of different characters on standard charts		
30.4	F.G Al.WG Oc.W.4s F.R Al.WR ★● DirWRG. 15-5M #	Direction light with narrow fairway sector flanked by light sectors of different characters on multicoloured charts		
31	▶ ⊙ Dir 286°	Moiré effect light (day and night), variable arrow mark. Arrows show when course alteration needed		475.8

		Sector Lights		
40.1	Fl.WRG.4s21m 18-12M	Sector light on standard charts		475 475.1 475.2 475.5
40.2	Fl.WRG.4s21m 18-12M #	Sector light on multicoloured charts		
41.1	Oc.WRG. 10-6M	Sector lights on standard charts, the white sector limits marking the sides of the fairway		475 475.1 475.5 470.4
41.2	Oc.WRG. 10-6M #	Sector lights on multicoloured charts, the white sector limits marking the sides of the fairway		
42	Fl(3)10s62m25M F.R.55m12M	Main light visible all-round with red subsidiary light seen over danger		471.8 475.4
43	Fl.5s41m30M	All-round light with obscured sector	Fl.5s41m30M	475.3
44	Iso.WRG	Light with arc of visibility deliberately restricted		475.3
45	Q.14m5M	Light with faint sector		475.3
46	Oc.R.8s / Oc.R.8s5M	Light with intensified sector		475.5
c		Light with unintensified sector	Oc.R.8s	Oc.R.8s5/2M

P Lights

Lights with limited Times of Exhibition				
50	☆ F.R(occas)	Lights exhibited only when specially needed (e.g. for fishing vessels, ferries) and some private lights	† (fishg.) † (Priv.) † (occasl.)	473.2
51	Fl.10s40m27M (F.37m11M Day) ☆	Daytime light (charted only where the character shown by day differs from that shown at night) †	Fl.10s40m27M (F.37m11M by Day) ☆	473.4
52	Q.WRG.5m10-3M (Fl.5s Fog) ☆	Fog light (exhibited only in fog, or character changes in fog) †	Q.WRG.5m10-3M Fl.5s (in Fog) ☆	473.5
53	☆ Fl.5s(U) †	Unwatched (unmanned) light with no standby or emergency arrangements		473.1
54	(temp) #	Temporary	† (temp) † (tempy.)	
55	(exting)	Extinguished	† (extingd.)	
b		Synchronized (synchronous or sequential)	(sync) or (sync)	

Special Lights	Flare Stack (at Sea) → L	Flare Stack (on Land) → E	Signal Stations → T	
60	☆ AeroAl.Fl.WG.7·5s11M	Aero light (may be unreliable)		476.1
61.1	☆ AeroF.R.353m11M RADIO MAST (353)	Air obstruction light of high intensity		476.2
61.2	(89) Λ (R Lts)	Air obstruction lights of low intensity †	(Red Lt.)	476.2
62	Fog Det Lt	Fog detector light		477
63	◁▷ (illuminated)	Floodlit, floodlighting of a structure	(illum) † (lit)	478.2
64	Iso F F.R	Strip light		478.5
65	☆ F.R (priv) #	Private light other than one exhibited occasionally	# ⊙ Y.Lt # ⊙ R.Lt † (Priv)	473.2

	IALA Maritime Buoyage System, which includes Beacons → Q 130			Buoys and Beacons	

			General	
1	—○—	Position of buoy or beacon		455.3 460.1 462.1

	Abbreviations for colours (lights) → P 11		Colour of Buoys and Beacon Topmarks	
2	G B G G G	Single colour; green (G) and black (B) †	B G	
3	R R Y Y Or R	Single colour other than green and black: red (R), yellow (Y), orange (Or) †	R Y Or	450 450.1 450.2 450.3 464 464.1 464.2 464.3
4	BY GRG BRB	Multiple colours in horizontal bands: the colour sequence is from top to bottom †	BW RW BR BW	
5	RW RW BuY RW	Multiple colours in vertical or diagonal stripes; the darker colour is given first. In these examples, red(R), white(W), blue (Bu), yellow (Y) & black(B) †	RW BR BW BW	
6		Retroreflecting material may be fitted to some unlit marks. Charts do not usually show it. Black bands will appear dark blue under a spotlight †	Refl	
a		Single colour other than green and black (non-IALA system: white (W) grey (Gy), blue (Bu)) †	W Gy Bu W (non-IALA) Gy (non-IALA) Bu (non-IALA)	464
b		Wreck buoy (not used in the IALA System) †	G G G G	
c		Chequered †	BR BW RW BW	

	Marks with Fog Signals → R		Lighted Marks	
7	Fl.G G Fl.R R	Lighted marks on standard charts (examples) †		457.1 466 466.1
8	Fl.R R Iso RW Fl.G G #	Lighted marks on multicoloured charts (examples)		

	For Application of Topmarks within the IALA System → Q 130 Radar reflector → S		Topmarks and Radar Reflectors		
9		IALA System buoy topmarks (beacon topmarks shown upright)	Non-IALA System # etc.		463 463.1
10	Name 2 R	Beacon with topmark, colour, radar reflector and designation (example)	"2" R	No.2 R	Ra.Refl "2" R †	450 455.2 455.7
11	Name 3 G	Buoy with topmark, colour, radar reflector and designation (example). Radar reflectors are not generally charted on IALA System buoys	"3" G	No.3 G	Ra.Refl "No.3" †	460.3 460.6 465.1 465.2

Q Buoys, Beacons

Buoys			*Features Common to Beacons and Buoys* → Q 1-11		

Shapes

20	⌂	▲	Conical buoy, nun buoy, ogival buoy	†	⌂ ▲ ▲ etc.	462.2
21	⌷	◣	Can buoy, cylindrical buoy	†	⌷ ◪ ◼ etc.	462.3
22	⌂	⌂	Spherical buoy	†	⌂ ⬙ ⬤ etc.	462.4
23	⚊	⚊	◢	Pillar buoy	†	⚊ ⚊	462.5
24	*I*		Spar buoy, spindle buoy	†	*I* ⊥ ℓ ℓ ⚊	462.6
25	⌂	◖	Barrel buoy, tun buoy	†		462.7
26	⌷		Superbuoy. Superbuoys are very large buoys, e.g. a LANBY (P6) is a navigational aid mounted on a circular hull of about 5m diameter. Oil or gas installation buoys (L16) and ODAS buoys (Q58), of similar size, are shown by variations of the superbuoy symbol	†	⌷	445.4 460.4 462.9 474

Minor Light Floats

30	⚓ Fl.G.3s Name	Light float as part of IALA System			462.8
31	⌷ Fl.10s	Light float not part of IALA System	†	🚩 🚩 🚩 🚩 🚩 B R B	462.8

Mooring Buoys

		Oil or Gas Installation Buoy → L		Visitors' (Small Craft) Mooring → U	
40	◖ # ⌂ # ⌷ # ◣	Mooring buoy		# ◼ # ⌂ # ⌷₁ † ⌷₁	431.5
41	◖ Fl.Y.2·5s	Lighted mooring buoy (example)			431.5 466.1 466.2 466.3 466.4
42		Trot, mooring buoys with ground tackle and berth numbers			323.1 431.6
43	◖ ∿∿∿∿∿∿∿∿	Mooring buoy with telegraphic or telephonic communications			431.5
44	Small Craft Moorings	Numerous moorings (example)			431.7

Buoys, Beacons   Q

The symbols shown below are examples: shapes of buoys may differ; lateral or cardinal buoys may be used in some situations; the use of the cross topmark is optional.

Special Purpose Buoys

50	DZ	Firing danger area (Danger Zone) buoy		441.2
51	Target	Target		
52	Marker Ship	Marker Ship		
53	Barge	Barge		
54	DG	Degaussing Range buoy		448.2
55	Cable	Cable buoy	Cable	443.6
56		Spoil ground buoy		446.3
57		Buoy marking outfall		444.4
58	ODAS	Data collection buoy (Ocean Data Acquisition System) of superbuoy size	ODAS	462.9
59		Buoy marking wave recorder or current meter		
60		Seaplane anchorage buoy		
61		Buoy marking traffic separation scheme		
62		Buoy marking recreation zone		
d		Racing mark		

Seasonal Buoys

70	(priv)	Buoy privately maintained (example)		
71	(Apr-Oct))	Seasonal buoy (the example shows a yellow spherical buoy on station between April and October)	# (1.4 -15.10) (occas)	460.5

Q Buoys, Beacons

130	IALA Maritime Buoyage System	*IALA International Association of Marine Aids to Navigation and Lighthouse Authorities*	NP 735

Where in force, the IALA System applies to all fixed and floating marks except landfall lights, leading lights and marks, sectored lights and major floating lights.

The standard buoy shapes are cylindrical (can) ⬠, conical △, spherical ◯, pillar 𝖎 , and spar 𝖎 , but variations may occur, for example: minor light floats ⊏▷

In the illustrations below, only the standard buoy shapes are used. In the case of fixed beacons (lit or unlit) only the shape of the topmark is of navigational significance.

130.1 Lateral marks *are generally for well-defined channels. There are two international Buoyage Regions - A and B - where Lateral marks differ.*

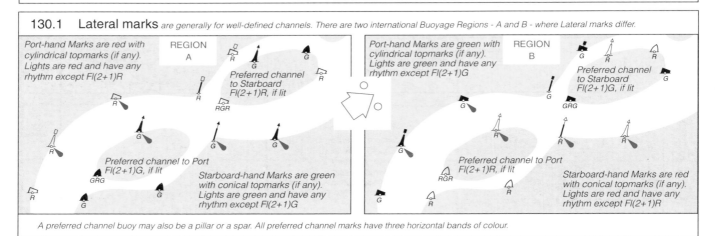

Port-hand Marks are red with cylindrical topmarks (if any). Lights are red and have any rhythm except Fl(2+1)R.

REGION A

Preferred channel to Starboard Fl(2+1)R, if lit

Preferred channel to Port Fl(2+1)G, if lit

Starboard-hand Marks are green with conical topmarks (if any). Lights are green and have any rhythm except Fl(2+1)G

Port-hand Marks are green with cylindrical topmarks (if any). Lights are green and have any rhythm except Fl(2+1)G

REGION B

Preferred channel to Starboard Fl(2+1)G, if lit

Preferred channel to Port Fl(2+1)R, if lit

Starboard-hand Marks are red with conical topmarks (if any). Lights are red and have any rhythm except Fl(2+1)R

A preferred channel buoy may also be a pillar or a spar. All preferred channel marks have three horizontal bands of colour.

130.2

Symbol showing direction of buoyage where not obvious.

Symbol showing direction of buoyage where not obvious, on multicoloured charts (red and green circles coloured as appropriate).

130.3 Cardinal Marks *indicating navigable water to the named side of the marks. Cardinal marks have the same meaning in Regions A and B*

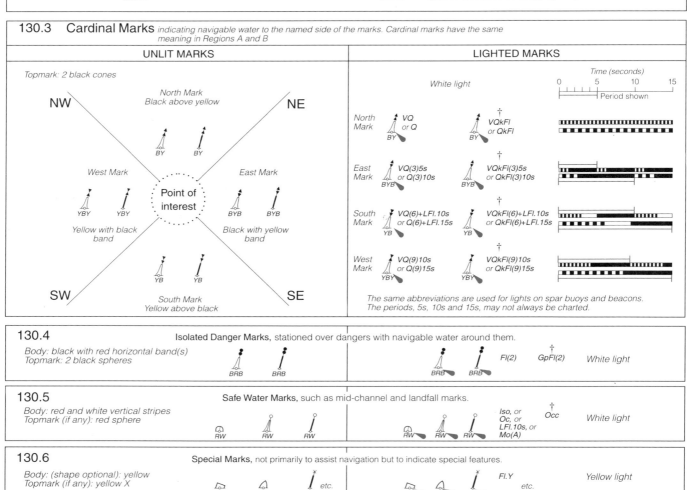

UNLIT MARKS

Topmark: 2 black cones

NW — North Mark, Black above yellow — NE

West Mark — Point of interest — East Mark

Yellow with black band — *Black with yellow band*

SW — South Mark, Yellow above black — SE

LIGHTED MARKS

White light

Time (seconds)
Period shown

North Mark	VQ or Q	VQkFl or QkFl
East Mark	VQ(3)5s or Q(3)10s	VQkFl(3)5s or QkFl(3)10s
South Mark	VQ(6)+LFl.10s or Q(6)+LFl.15s	VQkFl(6)+LFl.10s or QkFl(6)+LFl.15s
West Mark	VQ(9)10s or Q(9)15s	VQkFl(9)10s or QkFl(9)15s

The same abbreviations are used for lights on spar buoys and beacons. The periods, 5s, 10s and 15s, may not always be charted.

130.4 Isolated Danger Marks, *stationed over dangers with navigable water around them.*

Body: black with red horizontal band(s)
Topmark: 2 black spheres

Fl(2)   GpFl(2)   *White light*

130.5 Safe Water Marks, *such as mid-channel and landfall marks.*

Body: red and white vertical stripes
Topmark (if any): red sphere

Iso, or Oc, or LFl.10s, or Mo(A)   Occ   *White light*

130.6 Special Marks, *not primarily to assist navigation but to indicate special features.*

Body: (shape optional): yellow
Topmark (if any): yellow X

etc.   Fl.Y   etc.   *Yellow light*

				General
	Fog Detector Light → P	Fog Light → P		

1	((℗ ⚓ ⌂	Position of fog signal. Type of fog signal not stated	† Fog Sig	451 451.2 452.8

				Types of Fog Signals, Abbreviations
10	Explos	Explosive	† Gun	452.1
11	Dia	Diaphone		452.2
12	Siren	Siren		452.3
13	Horn	Horn (nautophone, reed, tyfon)	† Nauto † E.F. Horn † Tyfon † Reed	452.4
14	Bell	Bell		452.5
15	Whis	Whistle		452.6
16	Gong	Gong		452.7

				Examples of Fog Signal Descriptions
20	Fl.3s70m29M Siren Mo(N)60s	Siren at a lighthouse, giving a long blast followed by a short one (N), repeated every 60 seconds		452.3 453.3
21	Bell	Wave-actuated bell buoy. The provision of a legend indicating number of emissions, and sometimes the period, distinguishes automatic bell or whistle buoys from those actuated by waves		452.5 453 454.1
22	Q(6)+LFl.15s Horn(1)15sWhis YB	Light buoy, with horn giving a single blast every 15 seconds, in conjunction with a wave-actuated whistle	Reserve fog signals are fitted to certain buoys Only those actuated by waves are charted	452.4 453.1 454.3

‡ The Fog Signal symbol (R1) will usually be omitted when associated with another navigation aid (e.g. light or buoy) when a description of the signal is given

S Radar, Radio, Satellite Navigation Systems

Radar	Radar Structures Forming Landmarks → E		Radar Surveillance Systems → M		
1	⊙ Ra	Coast radar station providing range and bearing from station on request			485.1
2	⊙ Ramark	Ramark, radar beacon transmitting continuously			486.1
3.1	⊙ Racon(Z) (3cm)	Radar transponder beacon, with morse identification, responding within the 3cm (X) band	†	⊙ Racon(Z)	486.2 486.3
3.2	⊙ Racon(Z) (10cm)	Radar transponder beacon, with morse identification, responding within the 10cm (S) band			486.3
3.3	⊙ Racon(Z)	Radar transponder beacon, with morse identification, responding within the 3cm (X) and the 10cm (S) bands (or band unknown)	†	⊙ Racon(Z) (3 & 10cm)	
3.4	Racon Obscd / Racon(P)	Radar transponder beacon with sector of obscured reception			486.4
	Racon(Z) / Racon(Z)	Radar transponder beacon with sector of reception			
3.5	Racon ⊙ --- ⊙ Racon Racons ≠ 270	Leading radar transponder beacons (‡ and ‡ mean "in line")			486.5 433.3
	Racon ☆ --- ☆ Racon Lts ≠ 270 / Racons ≠ 270	Leading radar transponder beacons coincident with leading lights			
3.6	Racon Racon	Radar transponder beacons on floating marks (examples)			486.2
4	⅄	Radar reflector (not usually charted on IALA System buoys and buoyant beacons)	†	Ra.Refl.	460.3 465
5	⅄	Radar conspicuous feature	†	Ra conspic	485.2

52

Radar, Radio, Satellite Navigation Systems

Radio Structures Forming Landmarks → E		*Radio Reporting (Calling-in or Way) Points* → M			Radio
10 †	⊙ Name RC	Non-directional marine or aeromarine radiobeacon			481.1 480.1
11 †	⊙ RD ————— RD 269·5°	Directional radiobeacon with bearing line	† ⊙ Dir.Ro.Bn — — — — Dir.Ro.Bn 269°30′		481.2
†	☆----⊙☆--- Lts≠270° RD RD 270°	Directional radiobeacon coincident with leading lights			
12 †	⊙ RW	Rotating pattern radiobeacon			481.1
13 †	⊙ Consol	Consol beacon			481.3
14 †	⊙ RG	Radio direction-finding station	† ⊙ Ro.D.F		483
15 †	⊙ R	Coast radio station providing QTG service	† ⊙ Ro.		484
16 †	⊙ Aero RC	Aeronautical radiobeacon			482
17.1	⊙ AIS	Automatic Identification System transmitter			489.1
17.2	AIS AIS	Automatic Identification System transmitters on floating marks (examples)			489.1

				Satellite Navigation Systems	
50	WGS WGS72 WGS84	World Geodetic System, 1972 or 1984			201
Note:	*A note may be shown to indicate the shifts of latitude and longitude, to one, two or three decimal places of a minute, depending on the scale of the chart, which should be made to satellite-derived positions (which are referred to WGS84) to relate them to the chart. See Annual Notice to Mariners No.19.*				202
51	⊙ DGPS	Station providing Differential Global Positioning System corrections			481.5

53

LIVERPOOL JOHN MOORES UNIVERSITY
LEARNING SERVICES

T   Services

	Pilotage					
1.1	⬥		Pilot boarding place, position of pilot cruising vessel	† *Pilots*	† Pilots	
1.2	⬥ *Name*		Pilot boarding place, position of pilot cruising vessel, with name (e.g. District, Port)			491.1 491.2 491.6
1.3	⬥ *Note*		Pilot boarding place, position of pilot cruising vessel, with note (e.g. Tanker, Disembarkation)			
1.4	⬥ *H*		Pilots transferred by helicopter			491.2
2	■ Pilot lookout		Pilot office with Pilot lookout, Pilot lookout station			491.3
3	■ Pilots		Pilot office			491.4
4	**Port Name** (Pilots)		Port with pilotage service (boarding place not shown)			491.5

	Coastguard, Rescue				
10	■ CG ⊙ CG Ꝯ CG		Coastguard station	■ CGFS	492 492.1 492.2
11	■ CG♦ ⊙ CG♦ Ꝯ CG♦		Coastguard station with Rescue station	■ CGFS♦	493.3
12	♦		Rescue station, Lifeboat station, Rocket station	† LB	493 493.1
13	⛵♦ ♦		Lifeboat lying at a mooring		493.2
14	Ref		Refuge for shipwrecked mariners		456.4

			Stations		
20	⊙SS	Signal station in general	† Sig Sta	† Sig Stn	490.3
21	⊙SS(INT)	Signal station showing International Port Traffic Signals			495.5
22	⊙SS(Traffic)	Traffic signal station, Port entry and departure signals			495.1
23	⊙SS(Port Control)	Port control signal station			495.1
24	⊙SS(Lock)	Lock signal station			495.2
25.1	⊙SS(Bridge)	Bridge passage signal station			495.3
25.2	F. Traffic Sig	Bridge lights including traffic signals			495.4
26	⊙SS	Distress signal station			497
27	⊙SS	Telegraph station			497.1
28	⊙SS(Storm)	Storm signal station	† Storm Sig	† Stm. Sig. Stn.	494.1
29	⊙SS(Weather)	Weather signal station, Wind signal station			494.1
30	⊙SS(Ice)	Ice signal station			494.1
31	⊙SS(Time)	Time signal station			494.2
32.1	#	Tide scale or gauge	⊙Tide gauge		496.1
32.2	⊙Tide gauge	Automatically recording tide gauge			
33	⊙SS(Tide)	Tide signal station			496.2
34	⊙SS(Stream)	Tidal stream signal station			496.3
35	⊙SS(Danger)	Danger signal station			490.1
36	⊙SS(Firing)	Firing practice signal station			490.1

U Small Craft (Leisure) Facilities

Small Craft (Leisure) Facilities		Transport Features, Bridges →D Public Buildings, Cranes →F	Pilots, Coastguard, Rescue, Signal Stations →T	
1.1	⚓	Yacht harbour, Marina		320.2
1.2		Yacht berths without facilities	⚓	
2		Visitors´ berth	Ⓥ	
3		Visitors´ mooring	Ⓥ	
4		Yacht club, Sailing club	▸	
5		Public slipway	◣	
6		Boat hoist		
7		Public landing, Steps, Ladder	⌐	
8		Sailmaker		
9		Boatyard		
10		Public house, Inn	⊡	
11		Restaurant	✕	
12		Chandler		
13		Provisions		
14		Bank, Bureau de change		
15		Physician, Doctor		
16		Pharmacy, Chemist		
17		Water tap	ⵢ	
18		Fuel station (Petrol, Diesel)	⛽	
19		Electricity	ϟ	

20		Bottled gas		
21		Showers		
22		Laundrette	⊙	
23		Public toilets	**WC**	
24		Post box	📮	
25		Public telephone	☎	
26		Refuse bin	🗑	
27		Public car park	**P**	
28		Parking for boats and trailers	⊥	
29		Caravan site	🚐	
30		Camping site	△	
31		Water police		

| 32 | MARINA FACILITIES |

HARBOUR / MARINA FACILITIES	Diesel	Petrol	Bottled Gas	Electricity	Holding Tank Disposal	Repairs	Scrubbing Berth	Crane/Boat Hoist	Launching Slip	Pontoon Berthing	Swinging Moorings	Chandlery	Laundrette	Showers	VHF Radio Channels	Telephone Area Code	Telephone Number	Fax Number
FALMOUTH - Falmouth Visitors Yacht Haven				●						●	●	●		●	●	12	+44 (0) 1326	312285	211352
- Mylor Yacht Harbour	●	●	●	●	●	●	●	●	●	●	●	●	●	●	●	80/M	+44 (0) 1326	372121	372120
HELFORD - Helford Moorings Officer											●			●	●	-	+44 (0) 1326	250749	-

*Marina Facilities may be
tabulated on harbour charts and
large scale coastal charts.*
● *indicates that the facility is
available at the marina itself.
Laundrettes etc. located outside
the marina are not included. The
facilities may not be available
outside normal working hours. All
marinas have water, toilets and
rubbish disposal.*

Corrections

*Information on small craft (leisure) facilities will be updated as charts are revised by New Edition. The United Kingdom
Hydrographic Office would be pleased to receive reports of alterations or additions to small craft facilities.*

V Abbreviations of Principal Non-English Terms

Glossaries of non-English terms will be found in the volumes of Admiralty Sailing Directions.

On metric Admiralty charts, non-English terms are generally given in full wherever space and information permits. Where abbreviations are used on metric charts they accord with the following list, apart from those on charts published before 1980 where full stops are omitted. Obsolescent forms of abbreviations may also be found on these charts and on reproductions of other nations' charts.

CURRENT FORM	OBSOLESCENT FORM(S)	TERM	ENGLISH MEANING
ALBANIAN			
	K	Kodër, Kodra	*Hill*
ARABIC			
	Djeb, Dj	Djebel	*Mountain, Hill*
Geb.	G	Gebel	*Mountain, Hill*
J.	Jab, Jl	Jabal, Jibāl, Jebel	*Mountain(s), Hill(s)*
Jaz.	Jazt	Jazīrat, Jazā'ir Jazīreh	*Island(s), Peninsula*
Jeb.	J, Jl	Jebel	*Mountain, Hill*
Jez.	Jezt	Jezīrat	*Island, Peninsula*
Kh.	K	Khawr, Khōr	*Inlet, Channel*
	Si, Si	Sidi	*Tomb*
W.		Wād, Wādi	*Valley, River, River bed*
CHINESE			
Chg.	Chg	Chiang	*River, Shoal, Harbour, Inlet, Channel, Sound*
DANISH			
B.		Bugt	*Bay, Bight*
Bk.	Bk	Banke	*Bank*
Fj.	Fd	Fjord	*Inlet*
Gr.	Grd, Grd, Gd	Grund	*Shoal*
H.	Hm, Hm, Hne, Hne	Holm, Holmene	*Islet(s)*
Hd.	Hd	Hoved	*Headland*
Hn.	Hn	Havn, Havnen	*Harbour*
Ll.		Lille	*Little*
N.		Nord, Nordre	*North, Northern*
Ø.		Øst, Østre	*East, Eastern*
Øy.	Øne, Øne, Öne, Öne	Øyane, Øyene, Öyane Öyene	*Islands*
Pt.	Pt	Pynt	*Point*
S.		Sønder, Søndre	*South, Southern*
Sd.	Sd	Sund, Sundet	*Sound*
Sk.	Skr, Skr	Skær, Skjær	*Rock above water*
St.		Stor	*Great*
V.		Vest, Vestre	*West*
DUTCH			
B.	Bi	Baai	*Bay*
Bg.	Bg	Berg	*Mountain*
Bk.	Bk	Bank	*Bank*
Eil.	Eiln, Eiln	Eiland, Eilanden	*Island(s)*
G.		Golf	*Gulf*
	Gt, Grt, Gt, Grt	Groot, Groote	*Great*
H.		Hoek	*Cape, Hook*
Pt.	Pt	Punt	*Point*
R.		Rivier	*River*
Rf.	Rf	Rif	*Reef*
Str.	Stn, Str, Stn	Straat, Straten	*Strait(s)*
FINNISH			
K.		Kari, Kallio, Kivi	*Rock, Reef*
Lu.		Luoto, Luodet	*Rock(s)*
Ma.		Matala	*Shoal*
	P	Pieni, Pikku	*Small*
Sa.	Sa	Saari, Saaret	*Island(s)*
Tr.	Tr	Torni	*Tower*
FRENCH			
B.	Be	Baie	*Bay*
Bas.	B	Basse	*Shoal*
Bc.	Bc	Banc	*Bank*
	Bssn, Bn, Bn	Bassin	*Basin*
C.		Cap	*Cape*
Cal.	Chal, Chen	Chenal	*Channel*
Ch.	Chap, Chape	Chapelle	*Chapel*
Chât.	Châtu, Chau	Château	*Castle*

CURRENT FORM	OBSOLESCENT FORM(S)	TERM	ENGLISH MEANING
FRENCH *(continued)*			
F.	Fl	Fleuve	*Large river*
Ft.	Ft	Fort	*Fort*
G.		Golfe	*Gulf*
	Gd, Gd, Gde, Gde	Grand, Grande	*Great*
Ht.Fd.	H.F., Ht fd, Htfd, Ht fond	Haut-fond	*Shoal*
Î.	I, It	Île, Îles, Îlot	*Island(s), Islet*
L.		Lac	*Lake*
	Mn, Min	Moulin	*Mill*
Mlg.	Mge, Mage, Mou	Mouillage	*Anchorage*
Mt.	Mt	Mont	*Mount, Mountain*
	N.D.	Notre Dame	*Our Lady*
P.		Port	*Port*
	Pet, Pit, Pite, Pt	Petit, Petite	*Small*
Pit.	Pn, Pon	Piton	*Peak*
Pl.		Plage	*Beach*
Plat.	Pla, Platu	Plateau	*Tableland, Sunken flat*
Pte.	Pte	Pointe	*Point*
Qu.	Q	Quai	*Quay*
R.	Rau, Riv, Rau	Rivière, Ruisseau	*River, Stream*
	Rav, Rne	Ravine	*Ravine*
Rf.		Récif	*Reef*
Roc.	Re, Re, Rer, Rer	Roche, Rocher	*Rock*
S.	St, St, Ste, Ste	Saint, Sainte	*Saint, Holy*
	Som.	Sommet	*Summit*
Tr.	Tr	Tour	*Tower*
	Vi, Vx	Vieux, Vieil, Vielle	*Old*
GAELIC			
Bo.		Bogha	*Below water rock*
Eil.	E, En, En	Eilean, Eileanan	*Island(s), Islet(s)*
Ru.	Ru	Rubha	*Point*
Sg.	Sgr, Sgr	Sgeir	*Rock*
GERMAN			
B.		Bucht	*Bay*
Bg.	Bg	Berg	*Mountain*
Gr.	Grd, Grd, Gd	Grund	*Shoal*
Hn.	Hn	Hafen	*Harbour*
K.		Kap	*Cape*
Rf.	Rf	Riff	*Reef*
	Schl	Schloss	*Castle*
GREEK			
Ág., Ag.	Áy., Ay.	Ágios, Ágia	*Saint, Holy*
Ágk.	Ang.	Agkáli	*Bight, Open bay*
Ágky.	Angir., Ang	Agkyrovólio	*Anchorage*
Ák., Ak.		Ákra, Akrotírio	*Cape*
Kól.	Kol	Kólpos	*Gulf*
Lim.		Limín, Liménas	*Harbour*
N.		Nísos, Nísoi	*Island(s)*
N.	N	Nisída, Nisídes	*Islet(s)*
Ó.	O	Órmos	*Bay*
Or.		Ormískos	*Cove*
Ór.	Or	Óros, Óroi	*Mountain(s)*
Pot.		Potamós	*River*
	Prof	Profítis	*Prophet*
Sk.		Skópelos, Skópeloi	*Reef(s), Drying rock(s)*
Vrach.	Vrak	Vrachonisída, Vrachonisídes	*Rocky islets*
Vrach.	Vrák	Vráchos, Vráchol	*Rock(s)*
Yf.	Íf.	Ýfalos, Ýfaloi	*Reef(s)*
ICELANDIC			
Fj.	Fjr, Fdr	Fjörður	*Fjord*
Gr.		Grunn	*Shoal*

CURRENT FORM	OBSOLESCENT FORM(S)	TERM	ENGLISH MEANING
INDONESIAN and MALAY			
A.		Air, Ajer, Ayer	Stream
B.	Bu, B^u	Batu	Rock
Bat.	Btg, B^{tg}	Batang	River
	Bdr, B^{dr}	Bandar, Bendar	Port
	Br, B^r	Besar	Great
Buk.	Bt, B^t	Bukit	Hill
G.	Gg, G^g	Gosong, Gosung, Gusong, Gusung	Shoal, Reef, Islet
Gun.	Gg, G^g	Gunong, Gunung	Mountain
K.	Ki, K^i	Kali	River
K.	Kr	Kroeng, Krueng	River
Kam.	Kg, K^g	Kampong, Kampung	Village
Kar.	Kg, K^g	Karang	Coral reef, Reef
Kep.	Kpn, K^{pn}	Kepulauan	Archipelago
Kl.	K^l	Kachil, Kechil, Ketjil, Kecil	Small
Ku.	Kla, K^{la}	Kuala	River mouth
Lab.	Labn, Lab^n	Labuan, Labuhan	Anchorage, Harbour
Mu.	Ma, M^a	Muara	River mouth
P.	Pu, P^u, Po	Pulau, Pulu, Pulo	Island
Peg.		Pegunungan	Mountain range
Pel.	Pln, P^{ln}	Pelabuan, Pelabuhan	Roadstead, Anchorage
P.-P.	P.P.	Pulau-pulau	Group of islands
	Prt, P^{rt}	Parit	Stream, Canal, Ditch
S.	Si, S^i	Sungai, Sungei	River
Sel.	Slt, S^{lt}	Selat	Strait
T.	Tg, T^g	Tandjong, Tandjung, Tanjong, Tanjung, Tanjing	Cape
Tel.	Tal, Tk, T^k	Taluk, Telok, Teluk	Bay
U.	Ug, U^g	Udjung, Ujung	Cape
W.		Wai	River
ITALIAN			
Anc.		Ancoraggio	Anchorage
B.		Baia	Bay
Banch.	Bna, B^{na}	Banchina	Quay
Bco.	B^{co}	Banco	Bank
C.		Capo	Cape
Cal.		Calata	Wharf
Can.		Canale	Channel
Cas.		Castello	Castle
F.		Fiume	River
Fte.	F^{te}	Forte	Fort
G.		Golfo	Gulf
	Gde, G^{de}	Grande	Great
I.	I^a, I^e	Isola, Isole	Island(s)
I.	I^{to}, I^{ti}	Isolotto, Isolotti	Islet(s)
L.		Lago	Lake
Lag.	La, L^e	Laguna	Lagoon
	Mda, Mad, Mad^a, Mad^{na}	Madonna	Our Lady
Mte.	M^{te}	Monte	Mount, Mountain
P.	Pto, P^{to}	Porto	Port
P.	Portlo, Port^{lo}	Porticciolo	Small port
Pco.	P^{co}	Picco	Peak
Pog.	Pgio, P^{gio}	Poggio	Mound, Small hill
Pta.	P^{ta}	Punta	Point, Summit
	Pte, P^{te}	Ponte	Bridge
	Pzo, P^{zo}	Pizzo	Peak
S.	Sto, S^{to}, Sta, Sta	San, Santo, Santa	Saint, Holy
S.	SS, S.S.	Santi	Saints
Scog.	Sco, Sci, Sc, Sc^i	Scoglio, Scogli	Rock(s), Reef(s)
Scog.	Sc, Scra	Scogliera	Ridge of rocks, Breakwater
Sec.	Se	Secca, Secche	Shoal(s)
	T, T^{te}	Torrente	Intermittent stream
Tr.	Tre, T^{re}	Torre	Tower
	Va, V^{la}	Villa	Villa
JAPANESE			
B.	B^a	Bana	Cape, Point
By.	Bi, B^i	Byōchi	Anchorage
	D^e	Dake	Mountain, Hill
G.	G^a	Gawa	River
H.	Ha, H^a	Hana	Cape, Point
Hak.	Hi, H^i	Hakuchi	Roadstead

CURRENT FORM	OBSOLESCENT FORM(S)	TERM	ENGLISH MEANING
JAPANESE (continued)			
J.	J^a	Jima	Island
K.	Ka, K^a	Kawa	River
	Kaik, Ko, K^o	Kaikyō	Strait
M.	Mki, M^{ki}, M^i	Misaki	Cape
	Ma, M^a	Mura	Village
	Mi, M^i	Machi	Town
S.	Si, S^i	Saki	Cape, Point
Sh.	Sa, S^a	Shima	Island
	Sn, S^n	San	Mountain
	So, S^o	Seto	Strait
Su.	Sdo, S^{do}	Suidë	Channel
	Te, T^e	Take	Hill, Mountain
	Ya, Y^a	Yama	Mountain
Z.	Z^i	Zaki	Cape, Point
	Z^n	Zan	Mountain
MALAY (see INDONESIAN)			
NORWEGIAN			
B.	B, B^{kt}	Bukt, Bukta	Bay, Bight
Bg.	B^g	Berg, Bierg, Bjerg	Mountain, Hill
Fd.	F^d, Fj	Fjord, Fjorden	Fjord
Fjel.	Fj	Fjell, Fjellet, Fjeld, Fjeldet	Mountain
Fl.	Flne, F^{lne}	Flu, Flua, Fluen, Fluane, Fluene	Below water rock(s)
Gr.	Grne, Gr^{ne}	Grunn, Grunnen, Grunnane	Shoal(s)
H.	Hm, H^m, Hne, H^{ne}	Holm, Holmen, Holmane	Islet(s)
Hn.	H^n	Hamn, Havn	Harbour
in.	In^r, I	Indre, Inre, Inste	Inner
L.		Lille, Liten, Litla, Litle	Little
Lag.	La, L^a	Laguna	Lagoon
N.		Nord, Nordre	North, Northern
Ø.	Ö	Øst, Østre, Öst, Östre	East, Eastern
Od.	O	Odde, Odden	Point
Øy.	Ø, Ö, O	Øy, Øya, Öy, Öya	Island
Øy.	Øne, Ø^{ne}, Öne, Ö^{ne}	Øyane, Øyene, Öyane, Öyene	Islands
Pt.	P^t	Pynt, Pynten	Point
S.		Syd, Søre, Søndre	South, Southern
Sd.	S^d	Sund, Sundet	Sound
Sk.	Skr, Sk^r	Skjær, Skjer, Skjeret	Rock above water
Sk.	Skne, Sk^{ne}	Skjerane, Skjærane	Rocks above water
St.		Stor, Stora, Store	Great
Tar.	Tn, T^n	Taren	Below water rock
V.		Vest, Vestre	West
Vag.	Vg, V^g	Våg, Vågen	Bay, Cove
	Vd, V^d	Vand	Lake
Vik.	Vk, V^k	Vik, Vika, Viken	Bay, Inlet
	Vn, V^n	Vann, Vatn	Lake
Y.	Y^t	Ytre, Ytter, Yttre	Outer
PERSIAN			
B.		Bandar	Harbour
Jab.		Jabal	Mountain, Hill
Jaz.	Jazh, Jaz^h	Jazīreh	Island, Peninsu/a
Kh.	K	Khowr	Inlet, Channel
R.		Rūd	River
POLISH			
Jez.		Jezioro	Lake
Kan.		Kanal	Channel
Miel.		Mielizna	Shoal
R.		Rzeka	River
W.	Wys, Wa, W^a	Wyspa	Island
Zat.		Zatoka	Gulf, Bay
PORTUGUESE			
Anc.		Ancoradouro	Anchorage
Arq.	Arqu^o	Arquipélago	Archipelago
B.		Baía	Bay
Bco.	B^{co}	Banco	Bank
Bxo.	Ba, B^{xo}, Bxa, B^{xa}	Baixo, Baixa, Baixia, Baixio	Shoal
Co.	C.	Cabo	Cape

PORTUGUESE (continued)

CURRENT FORM	OBSOLESCENT FORM(S)	TERM	ENGLISH MEANING
Can.		Canal	Channel
Ens.	Ens^a	Enseada	Bay, Creek
Est.	Est^o	Esteiro	Creek, Inlet
Estr.		Estreito	Strait
Estu.	Est, Est^o	Estuario	Estuary
Fte.	F^{te}	Forte	Fort
Fte.	Ftza, F^{tza}	Fortaleza	Fortress
Fund.		Fundeadouro	Anchorage
G.		Golfo	Gulf
	Gde, G^{de}	Grande	Great
I.		Ilhéu, Ilhéus, Ilhota	Islet(s)
I.		Ilha, Ilhas	Island(s)
L.		Lago	Lake
L.		Lagoa	Small lake, Marsh
La.	Le, L^e	Laje	Flat-topped rock
Lag.	La, L^a	Laguna	Lagoon
Mol.	Me, M^e	Molhe	Mole
Mor.	Mo, M^o	Morro	Headland, Hill
Mt.	M^{te}, Mte	Monte, Montanha	Mount, Mountain
NS.	Na.Sa, N^{a}S^a	Nosso Senhor, Nossa Senhora	Our Lord, Our Lady
P.	Pto, P^{to}	Porto	Port
Pal.	Pals, Pal^s	Palheiros	Fishing village
Par.	Pel, P^{el}	Parcel	Shoal, Reef
Pass.	Pas	Passagem, Passo	Passage, Pass
	Pco, P^{co}, P^o	Pico	Peak
Pda.	P^{da}	Pedra	Rock
	Peq	Pequeno, Pequena	Small
Pr.	Pa, P^a	Praia	Beach
Pta.	P^{ta}	Ponta	Point
Queb.		Quebrada, Quebrado	Cut, Ravine
Rch.		Riacho, Ribeira, Ribeirão	Creek, Stream, River
Rf.		Recife	Reef
Ro.	R	Rio	River
Roc.	Ra, R^a	Rocha, Rochedo	Rock
S.	Sto, S^{to}, Sta, Sta	São, Santo, Santa	Saint, Holy
Sa.	Sa, S^a, Sr	Serra, Cordilheira	Mountain range
	Va, V^a	Vila	Town, Village, Villa

ROMANIAN

CURRENT FORM	OBSOLESCENT FORM(S)	TERM	ENGLISH MEANING
A.		Ansă, Ansa	Cove
B.		Baie, Baia	Bay
Br.		Braţ, Braţul, Braţu	Branch, Arm (of the sea)
C.		Cap, Capul, Capu	Cape
Di., D-le.		Deal, Dealul, Dealuri, Dealurile	Hill(s)
Fd.mic		Fund mic	Shoal
I.		Insulă, Insula	Island
L.		Lac, Lacul, Lacu	Lake
Mt., M-ţii.		Munte, Muntele, Munţi, Muntii	Mountain, Mounts
O.		Ostrov, Ostrovul, Ostrovu	Island
S.		Stîncă, Stînca	Rock
Sf.		Sfint, Sfintu, Sfintul, Sfinta	Saint, Holy
Str.		Strîmtoare, Strîmtoarea	Pass, Strait

RUSSIAN

CURRENT FORM	OBSOLESCENT FORM(S)	TERM	ENGLISH MEANING
B		Bukhta	Bay, Inlet
b-ka.	Bka, B^{ka}, Bki, B^{ki}, Bk	Banka, Banki	Bank(s)
Bol.		Bol'shoy, Bol'shaya, Bol'shoye	Great, Large
Gb.	G, Ga, G^a	Guba	Gulf, Bay, Inlet
G.		Gora	Mountain, Hill
Gav.	G	Gavan'	Harbour, Basin
Kam.		Kamen'	Rock
M.		Mys	Cape, Headland
	Mal	Malyy, Malaya, Maloye	Little
O.	O^{va}	Ostrov, Ostrova	Island(s)
Oz.		Ozero	Lake
P-ov.	Pol^{ov}, P^{ov}, Pol	Poluostrov	Peninsula
Pr.	Prv, Pr^v	Proliv	Channel, Strait
R.		Reka	River
Zal.		Zaliv	Gulf, Bay

SPANISH

CURRENT FORM	OBSOLESCENT FORM(S)	TERM	ENGLISH MEANING
A.	Arro, Arr^o	Arroyo	Stream
Arch.	Arch^o	Archipiélago	Archipelago
Arrf.	Arr^e, Arr^{fe}, Arr	Arrecife	Reef
Ba.	B^a	Bahía	Bay
Bo.	B^o	Bajo	Shoal
Bco.	B^{co}	Banco	Bank
Br.	Bzo, B^{zo}	Rompientes	Breakers
C.		Cabo	Cape
Cal.	Cta	Caleta	Cove
Can.		Canal	Channel
Cer.	Co, C^o	Cerro	Hill
Cre.		Cumbre, Cima	Summit
	Cy	Cayo	Cay, Key
Ens.	Ens^a	Ensenada	Bay, Creek
Est.	Est^o	Estero	Creek, Inlet
Estr.		Estrecho	Strait
Estu.	Est, Est^o	Estuario	Estuary
Fond.	Fond^o	Fondeadero	Anchorage
Fte.	F^{te}	Fuerte	Fort
G.		Golfo	Gulf
	Gde, G^{de}	Grande	Great
I.	J^a	Isla, Islas	Island(s)
I.	J^{te}	Islote, Isleta	Islet
L.		Lago	Lake
Lag.	La, L^a	Laguna	Lagoon
Mor.	Mo, M^o	Morro	Headland, Hill
Mte.	M^{te}	Monte	Mount, Mountain
Mu.	Me, M^e, Mlle	Muelle	Mole
	Na. Sa, N^{a}S^a	Nuestra Señora	Our Lady
P.	Pto, P^{to}	Puerto	Port
Pco.	P^{co}, P^o	Pico	Peak
Pda.	P^{da}	Piedra	Rock
Pen.	Pen^{la}	Península	Peninsula
	Peq	Pequeño, Pequeña	Small
Pl.	Pa, P^a	Playa	Beach
Prom.	Prom^{to}	Promontorio	Promontory
Pta.	P^{ta}	Punta	Point
Queb.		Quebrada	Cut, Ravine
R.		Río	River
Rga.		Restinga	Shoal, Sandbank
Roc.	Ra, R^a	Roca	Rock
S.	Sn, S^n, Sto, S^{to}, Sta, Sta	San, Santo, Santa	Saint, Holy
Sr.	Sa, S^a	Sierra	Mountain range
Surg.	Surgo, Surg^o	Surgidero	Anchorage, Roadstead
Tr.	T^{re}	Torre	Tower
	Va, V^a	Villa	Villa, Small town

SWEDISH

CURRENT FORM	OBSOLESCENT FORM(S)	TERM	ENGLISH MEANING
B.		Bukt	Bay, Bight
Bg.	Bgt, B^g	Berg, Berget	Mountain
	Bk, B^k	Bank	Bank
Fj.	F^d	Fjärd, Fjord	Fjord
	Gla, G^{la}	Gamla	Old
Gr.	Grn, Grd, Grd, G^d	Grund	Shoal
H.	Hm, H^m	Holme, Holmarna	Islet
	Hd, H^d	Huvud	Headland
	Hn, H^n	Hamn, Hamnen	Harbour
I.		Inre	Inner
L.		Lilla, Liten	Little, Small
N.		Nord, Norra	North, Northern
Ö.		Öst, Östra	East, Eastern
S.		Syd, Södra	South, Southern
Sk.	Sk^r	Skär, Skäret, Skären	Rock above water
St.		Stor	Great, Large
V.		Väst, Västra	West, Western
Y.	Y^t	Yttre	Outer

THAI

CURRENT FORM	OBSOLESCENT FORM(S)	TERM	ENGLISH MEANING
Kh.		Khao	Hill, Mountain
L.	Lm, L^m	Laem	Cape, Point
M.N.		Mae Nam	River

TURKISH

CURRENT FORM	OBSOLESCENT FORM(S)	TERM	ENGLISH MEANING
Ad.		Ada, Adası	Island
Aşp		Takimadalar	Archipelago
Adc.	Ad	Adacık	Islet
Boğ.		Boğaz, Boğazı	Strait
Br.	Bn, Bu	Burun, Burnu	Point, Cape
Ç.	Ça	Çay, Çayı	Stream, River

CURRENT FORM	OBSOLESCENT FORM(S)	TERM	ENGLISH MEANING
		TURKISH *(continued)*	
D.	Da De	Dağ, Dağı	*Mountain*
Dz.		Dere, Deresi	*Valley, Stream*
G.		Deniz	*Sea*
Isk.		Göl, Gölü	*Lake*
Kf. Krf.		İskele, İskelesi	*Jetty*
Ky.	Kyl.	Körfez, Körfezi	*Gulf*
Lim. Lm.	Li	Kaya, Kayası	*Rock*
N.		Liman, Limanı	*Harbour*
		Nehir, Nehri, Irmak, Irmağı	*River*
T.	Te, Te	Tepe, Tepesi	*Hill, Peak*
Yad.		Yarımada, Yarımadası	*Peninsula*

CURRENT FORM	OBSOLESCENT FORM(S)	TERM	ENGLISH MEANING
		Languages of the former YUGOSLAVIA	
Br.		Brdo, Brda	*Mountain(s)*
Gr.		Greben, Grebeni	*Rock, Reef, Cliff, Ridge*
Hr.		Hrid, Hridi	*Rock*
L.		Luka	*Harbour, Port*
M.		Mali, Mala, Malo, Malen	*Small*
O.		Otočić, Otočići	*Islet(s)*
O.		Otok, Otoci	*Island(s)*
Pl.		Pličina	*Shoal*
Pr.		Prolaz	*Passage*
S.	Sv	Sveti, Sveta, Sveto	*Saint, Holy*
Šk.		Školj, Školjić	*Island, Reef*
U.		Uvala, Uvalica	*Inlet*
V.		Veli, Vela, Velo, Velik, Veliki, Velika, Veliko	*Great*
Z.	Zal	Zaliv, Zaljev, Zaton	*Gulf, Bay*

CURRENT FORM	OBSOLESCENT FORM(S)	TERM	REFERENCES
abt	ab^t	About	O a
Aero		Aeronautical	P 60, 61
	Al	Algae	J t
Al.	Alt	Alternating light	P 10.11
ALC		Articulated Loading Column	L 12
ALL		Admiralty List of Lights and Fog Signals	—
ALRS		Admiralty List of Radio Signals	—
Am		Amber	P 11.8
Anch.	Anch^e	Anchorage	O 21
	Anct, Anc^t	Ancient	O 84
ANM		Annual Summary of Admiralty Notices to Mariners	—
Annly	Ann^{ly}	Annually	—
Appr.	Apprs, Appr^s	Approaches	O 22
approx	Approx	Approximate	O 89
Apr		April	—
Arch.	Archo, Arch^o	Archipelago	G 5
ASD		Admiralty Sailing Directions	—
ASL		Archipelagic Sea Lane	M17
	Astr, Astrl, Astr^l	Astronomical	—
ATBA		Area to be Avoided	M14, 29
ATT		Admiralty Tide Tables	—
Aug		August	—
Aus		Australia	—
Ave	Av^e	Avenue	G 111
B.		Bay	O 4
B	bl, blk	Black	J af, Q 2
	Ba	Basalt	J i
	Batt, Baty, Bat^y	Battery	E 34.3
Bk.	B^k	Bank	O 23
bk	brk	Broken	J 33
Bldg	B^{ldg}	Building	D 5
	BM, B.M.	Bench Mark	B 23
Bn, Bns		Beacon(s)	M 1-2, P 4-5, Q 80-81
BnTr	Bn Tower	Beacon Tower	P 3, Q 110
	Bo	Boulders	J e
Bol	Boll.	Bollard	F a, G 181
Br		Breakers	K 17
	br	Brown	J ak
Bu	Bl, Bl., b	Blue	J ag, P 11.4, Q a
C.		Cape	G 7
c		Coarse	J 32
ca	cal	Calcareous	J 38
CALM		Catenary Anchor Leg Mooring	L 16
Cas	Cas.	Castle	E 34.2, G 64
	Cath, Cath.	Cathedral	E 10.1, G 75
Cb		Cobbles	J 8
cd		Candela	B 54
CD		Chart Datum	H 1
	Cemy, Cem^y	Cemetery	E 19
CG	C.G.	Coastguard station	T 10-11
Ch	Ch.	Church, chapel	E 10.1, E 11
	ch, choc	Chocolate	J al
Chan.		Channel	O 14
Chem		Chemical	L 40
	chk, Ck	Chalk	J f
Chy	Ch^y	Chimney	E 22
	cin, Cn	Cinders	J n
cm	cm.	Centimetre(s)	B 43
Co	crl	Coral	J 10, K 16
	Col	Column, pillar, obelisk	E 24, G 66
	conspic	Conspicuous	E 2
const	constn, constr^n	Construction	F 32
cov	cov.	Covers	K c
Cr.		Creek	O 7
Cup	Cup.	Cupola	E 10.4
Cy	cl	Clay	J 3
	(D)	Doubtful	—
	d	Dark	J ao
Dec		December	—
decrg	decr^g	Decreasing	B 64
dest	destd, Dest^d	Destroyed	O 93
Det		(see Fog Det Lt)	—
DG, DG Range	D. G. Range	Degaussing Range	N 25, Q 54
DGPS		Differential Global Positioning System	S 51
	Di, di	Diatoms	J w
Dia		Diaphone	R 11

CURRENT FORM	OBSOLESCENT FORM(S)	TERM	REFERENCES
Dir	Dir^n	Direction	—
Dir	Dir Lt	Directional light	P 30-31
Discol	Discol^d	Discoloured water	K e
discont	discontd, discont^d	Discontinued	O b
dist	Dist	Distant	O 85
Dk	D^k	Dock	G c
dm	dm.	Decimetre(s)	B 42
Dn, Dns	D^n	Dolphin(s)	F 20
dr	dr., Dr.	Dries	K b
DW		Deep-water, Deep-draught	M 27, N 12.4
dwt		Deadweight tonnage	—
DZ		Danger Zone	Q 50
E	E.	East	B 10
ED	(ED), (E.D.)	Existence doubtful	I 1
EEZ		Exclusive Economic Zone	N 47
	E.F. Horn	Electric fog horn	R 13
Ent.	Entce, Ent^{ce}	Entrance	O 16
	Equin^l	Equinoctial	—
ESSA		Environmentally Sensitive Sea Area	N 22
Est.	Est^y	Estuary	O 17
	Estab^t	Establishment	—
	ev.	Every	—
exper	experl, Exper^l	Experimental	O 92
explos	explos.	Explosive	R 10
(exting)	(exting^d)	Extinguished	P 55
f		Fine	J 30
F		Fixed light	P 10.1
FAD		Fish Aggregating Device	—
F Racon		Fixed frequency radar transponder beacon	S 3.4
Feb		February	—
FFL		Fixed and flashing light	P 10.10
Fj.	Fd, F^d (fish^g)	Fjord	O 5
		Fishing light	P 50
Fl	fl.	Flashing light	P 10.4
	Fl., fl	Flood	—
Fla		Flare stack (at sea)	L 11
	Fm, F^m	Farm	G 53
fm, fms	f^m, f^{ms}	Fathom, fathoms	B 48
Fog Det Lt		Fog detector light	P 62
	Fog Sig.	Fog signal station	R 1
	Fog W/T	Radio fog signal	—
FPSO		Floating Production and Storage Offtake Vessel	L17
	Fr, for	Foraminifera	J u
FS	F.S.	Flagstaff, Flagpole	E 27
FSO		Floating Storage and Offtake Vessel	L17
	Ft, F^t	Fort	E 34.2
ft	f^t	Foot, feet	B 47, P 13
G	g	Gravel	J 6
G	gn	Green	J ah, P 11.3, Q 2
G.		Gulf	O 3
	ga, glac	Glacial	J ac
	Gc	Glauconite	J p
	Gd, grd	Ground	J a
	Gl, gl	Globigerina	J v
	Govt Ho, Gov^t Ho	Government House	—
Gp.		Group (of islands)	—
	GpFl, Gp.Fl.	Group-flashing light	P 10.4
	GpOcc, Gp.Occ.	Group-occulting light	P 10.2
GPS		Global Positioning System	—
grt		Gross Register Tonnage	—
	Gt, Grt, G^t, Gr^t	Great	—
	G.T.S.	Great Trigonometrical Survey Station (India)	—
	Gy, gy	Grey	J am, Q a
GT		Gross Tonnage	—
h		Hard	J 39
	H, H.	Headway	D 20, D 26-27
H		Helicopter transfer (Pilots)	T 1.4
h	h., H.	Hour	B 49
HAT		Highest Astronomical Tide	H 3
Hd.	H^d	Headland	G 8
Hn.	H^n	Haven	G 139
Ho		House	G 61
(hor)	(hor^l)	Horizontally disposed	P 15
Hosp	Hospl, Hosp^l	Hospital	F 62.2
Hr.	H^r	Harbour	G 138
	Hr, H^r	Higher	—
Hr Mr		Harbour Master	F 60
	Ht, H^t	Height	—

CURRENT FORM	OBSOLESCENT FORM(S)	TERM	REFERENCES
HW	H.W.	High Water	H a
	H.W.F. & C.	High Water Full and Change	—
	H.W.O.S.	High Water Ordinary Springs	—
I.	It	Island, islet	G 1-2
IALA		International Association of Lighthouse Authorities	Q 130
IHO		International Hydrographic Organization	—
(illum)	Illum., (lit)	Illuminated	P 63
IMO		International Maritime Organization	—
	in., ins.	Inch, inches	—
incrg	incr^g	Increasing	B 65
INT		International	A 3, T 21
Intens	(intens)	Intensified	P 46
IQ	IntQkFl, Int.Qk.Fl.	Interrupted quick-flashing light	P 10.6
	(irreg.)	Irregular	—
	ISLW, I.S.L.W.	Indian Spring Low Water	—
Iso		Isophase light	P 10.3
	It	Islet	G 2
ITZ		Inshore Traffic Zone	—
IUQ		Interrupted ultra quick-flashing light	P 10.8
IVQ	IntVQkFl, Int.V.Qk.Fl	Interrupted very quick-flashing light	P 10.7
Jan		January	—
Jul		July	—
km	km.	Kilometre(s)	B 40, F 40
kn	kn.	Knot(s)	B 52, H 40-41
L.		Lake, Loch, Lough	O 6
	l	Large	J ab
Lag.	Lagn, Lag^n	Lagoon	G 13, O 8
LANBY		Large Automatic Navigational Buoy	P 6
LASH		Lighter Aboard Ship	G 184
LAT		Lowest Astronomical Tide	H 2
Lat	Lat.	Latitude	B 1
	LB, L.B.	Lifeboat station	T 12
Ldg	L^{dg}	Leading	P 20.3
Le.	L^e	Ledge	O 28
LFl		Long-flashing light	P 10.5
	Lit, Lit.	Little	—
	(lit)	Floodlit	P 63
LL	L.L.	List of Lights	—
Lndg.	L^{dg}	Landing place	F 17
LNG		Liquefied Natural Gas	G 185
LOA		Length overall	—
LoLo		Load-on, Load-off	—
Long	Long.	Longitude	B 2
LPG		Liquefied Petroleum Gas	G 186
	Lr, L^r	Lower	P 23
	L.S.S.	Lifesaving station	—
Lt	L^t, It	Light	J an, P 1
Lts		Lights	P 20.1, 61.2
LtHo	L^t Ho	Lighthouse	P 1
Lt V	L^t V	Light-vessel	P 6
	Lv, lv	Lava	J j
LW	L.W.	Low Water	H b
	L.W.F. & C.	Low Water Full and Change	—
	L.W.O.S.	Low Water Ordinary Springs	—
M	m	Mud	J 2
M	M.	Sea Mile(s)	B 45, P 14
m		Medium	J 31
m	m.	Metre(s)	B 41, P 13
	mad, Md	Madrepore	J h
Mag	Mag.	Magnetic	B 61
	Magz, Mag^z	Magazine	—
	man, Mn	Manganese	J o
Mar		March	—
MHHW	M.H.H.W.	Mean Higher High Water	H 13
MHLW	M.H.L.W.	Mean Higher Low Water	H 14

CURRENT FORM	OBSOLESCENT FORM(S)	TERM	REFERENCES
MHW		Mean High Water	H 5
MHWN	M.H.W.N.	Mean High Water Neaps	H 11
MHWS	M.H.W.S.	Mean High Water Springs	H 9
	Mid, Mid.	Middle	—
min	min., m.	Minute(s) of time	B 50
Mk		Mark	Q 101
	Ml, ml	Marl	J c
LHW	M.L.H.W.	Mean Lower High Water	H 15
MLLW	M.L.L.W.	Mean Lower Low Water	H 12
MLW		Mean Low Water	H 4
MLWN	M.L.W.N.	Mean Low Water Neaps	H 10
MLWS	M.L.W.S.	Mean Low Water Springs	H 8
mm	mm.	Millimetre(s)	B 44
Mo		Morse code	P 10.9, R 20
Mon	Mont, Mon^t	Monument	E 24
	Mony, Mon^y	Monastery	G 76
	Ms, mus	Mussels	J r
MSL	M.S.L.	Mean Sea Level	H 6
Mt.	M^t	Mountain, mount	G 23
Mth.	Mth	Mouth	O 19
MTL	M.T.L.	Mean Tide Level	H c
N	N.	North	B 9
	Nauto	Nautophone	R 13
NB	N.B.	Notice Board	Q 126
NE	N.E.	North-east	B 13
NM	N.M.	Notice(s) to Mariners	—
n mile		International Nautical Mile	B 45
No	N^o	Number	N 12.2
Nov		November	—
Np	Np.	Neap Tides	H 17
nrt		Nett register tonnage	—
NT		Net Tonnage	—
NW	N.W	North-west	B 15
NZ		New Zealand	—
	Obs Spot, Obsn Spot, Obs^n Spot	Observation Spot	B 21
Obscd	Obsc^d	Obscured	P 43
Obstn	Obst^n	Obstruction, Diffuser	K 40-43, L 43
	Obsy, Obs^y	Observatory	G 73
Oc	Occ, Occ.	Occulting light	P 10.2
(occas)	(occas^l)	Occasional	P 50
Oct		October	—
OD	O.D.	Ordnance Datum	H d
ODAS		Ocean Data-Acquisition System	Q 58
	Off, Off.	Office	G 72
Or	Or.	Orange	P 11.7, Q 3
	ord.	Ordinary	—
	Oy, oys	Oysters	J q
	Oz, oz	Ooze	J b
P	peb	Pebbles	J 7
P.		Port	G 137
(P)		Preliminary (NM)	—
PA	(PA), (P.A.)	Position approximate	B 7
Pag	Pag.	Pagoda	E 14
Pass.		Passage	O 13
PD	(PD), (P.D.)	Position doubtful	B 8
Pen.	Penla, Pen^{la}	Peninsula	G 4
Pk.	p^k	Peak	G 25
	Pm, pum	Pumice	J k
PO	P.O.	Post Office	F 63
	Po, pol	Polyzoa	J z
pos	posn, pos^n	Position	—
(priv)	priv., (Priv.)	Private	P 50, P 65, Q 70
Prod Well		Production Well	L 20
prohib	Prohib^d	Prohibited	O c
proj	projd, Proj^d	Projected	O 80
prom	promt, Prom^t	Prominent	O d
Prom.	Promy, Prom^y	Promontory	G 20
	(prov), (prov^l)	Provisional	—
PSSA		Particularly Sensitive Sea Area	—
Pt.	P^t	Point	G 9
	Pt, pt	Pteropods	J y
Pyl		Pylon	D 26
Q	QkFl, Qk.Fl.	Quick-flashing light	P 10.6
	Q^r	Quarter	—
	Qz, qrtz	Quartz	J g
R	rd	Red	J aj, P 11.2, Q 3
R.		River	

CURRENT FORM	OBSOLESCENT FORM(S)	TERM	REFERENCES
R	r	Rock	J 9, K 15
R	R^o	Coast Radio Station providing QTG service	S 15
Ra		Radar Range, Radar Reference Line, Coast Radar Station	M 31–32, S 1
	Ra (conspic), Ra. (conspic)	Radar conspicuous object	S 5
	Ra. Refl.	Radar Reflector	Q 10–11, S 4
Racon		Radar Transponder Beacon	S 3
	rad, Rd	Radiolaria	J x
Ramark		Radar Beacon	S 2
RC		Non-directional Radio-beacon	S 10
RD	Dir.Ro.Bn	Directional Radiobeacon	S 11
Rds.	R^{ds}	Roads, Roadstead	O 20
Ref		Refuge	Q 124, T 14
Refl	Refl.	Retroreflecting material	Q 6
	Rem^{ble}	Remarkable	—
Rep	Repd, Rep^d	Reported	I 3
Rf.	R^f	Reef	O 26
RG	R^o D.F.	Radio Direction-Finding Station	S 14
Rk.	R^k	Rock	G 11
(R Lts)	(Red Lts)	Air Obstruction Lights (low intensity)	P 61.2
	Rly, Ry, R^y	Railway	D 13
	R^o B^n	Radiobeacon in general	S 10
RoRo	Ro-Ro	Roll-on Roll-off ferry terminal	F 50
	R.S.	Rocket station	—
Ru, (ru)	Ru.	Ruins	D 8, E 25.2, F 33
RW		Rotating Pattern Radiobeacon	S 12
S.	St, S^t	Saint	G 54
S	s	Sand	J 1
S	S.	South	B 11
s	sec, sec.	Second(s) of time	B 51, P 12
SALM		Single Anchor Leg Mooring	L 12
SBM		Single Buoy Mooring	L 16
SC	S.C.	Sailing Club	U 4
	Sc, sc	Scoriæ	J m
Sc	Sc.	Scanner	E 30.3
Sch	Sch.	School	G b
SD	S.D.	Sailing Directions	—
SD		Sounding of doubtful depth	I 2
Sd.	S^d	Sound	O 12
SE	S.E.	South–east	B 14
	Sem, Sem.	Semaphore	—
Sep		September	—
sf	stf	Stiff	J 36
Sh	sh	Shells	J 11
Sh.		Shoal	O 25
Si		Silt	J 4
Sig	Sig.	Signal	R 1, T 25.2
	sk, spk	Speckled	J ad
	sm	Small	J aa
SMt	SM^t	Seamount	O 33
	Sn, shin	Shingle	J d
so	sft	Soft	J 35
Sp	Sp.	Spire	E 10.3
	Sp, sp	Sponge	J s
Sp	Sp, Spr.	Spring Tides	H 16
SPM		Single Point Mooring	L 12
SS	Sig Sta, Sig Stn	Signal Station	T 20–36
St	st	Stones	J 5
St	St.	Street	G 110
Sta	Sta., Stn, St^n	Station	D 13
	Stm.Sig.Stn.	Storm Signal Station	T 28
Str.		Strait	O 11
subm	submd, $Subm^d$	Submerged	O 90
SW	S.W.	South-west	B 16
SWOPS		Single Well Oil Production System	L c
sy	stk	Sticky	J 34
	T, t	Tufa	J 1
(T)		Temporary (NM)	—
t		Ton, tonne	B 53, F 53
	t	Elevation of top of trees	C 14
Tel	Tel.	Telephone, Telegraph	G 95
(temp)	(tempy), $(temp^y)$	Temporary	N b, P 54
Tr	T^r	Tower	E 10.2, E 20

CURRENT FORM	OBSOLESCENT FORM(S)	TERM	REFERENCES
TSS		Traffic Separation Scheme	—
TV Tr	T.V. T^r	Television Tower	E 28–29
	(U)	Unwatched, unmanned (light)	P 53
ULCC		Ultra Large Crude Carrier	—
uncov	uncov.	Uncovers	K d
unexam	unexamd. $unexam^d$	Unexamined	I a
Unintens		Unintensified	P a
	Up^r	Upper	P 22
UQ		Ultra quick-flashing light	P 10.8
UTC		Co-ordinated Universal Time	—
UTM		Universal Transverse Mercator	—
v	vol	Volcanic	J 37
	Va, V^a	Villa	—
Var	Var^n	Variation	B 60
	var	Varying	—
Vel	Vel.	Velocity	—
(vert)	$(vert^l)$	Vertically disposed	P 15
Vi		Violet	P 11.5
	vis.	Visible	—
VLCC		Very Large Crude Carrier	G 187
Vol.		Volcano	G 26
VQ	VQkFl, V.Qk.Fl	Very quick-flashing light	P 10.7
VTS		Vessel Traffic Service	—
W	W.	West	B 12
W	w	White	J ae, P 11.1, Q a
Water Tr	Water T^r	Water tower	E 21
Wd	wd	Weed	J 13.1
WGS		World Geodetic System	S 50
Whf	Wh^f	Wharf	F 13, G d
Whis	Whis.	Whistle	R 15
Wk	W^k	Wreck	K 20–30
	W/T	Radio (Wireless/Telegraphy)	—
Y	y	Yellow, amber, orange	J ai, P 11, IQ 3
YC	Y.C.	Yacht Club	U 4
	y^d, y^{ds}	Yard(s)	—

International Abbreviations W

A		
Aero	Aeronautical light	P 60, 61.1
† Aero RC	Aeronautical radiobeacon	S 16
AIS	Automatic Identification System	S 17
Al	Alternating	P 10.11
ALC	Articulated Loading Column	L 12
Am	Amber	P 11.8
ASL	Archipelagic Sea Lane	M 17

B		
B	Black	Q 2, 81
bk	Broken	J 33
Bn	Beacon	P 4, 5, Q 80
BnTr	Beacon tower	P 3, Q 110
Bo	Boulder(s)	J 9.2
Br	Breakers	K 17
Bu	Blue	P 11.4

C		
c	Coarse	J 32
ca	Calcareous	J 38
CALM	Catenary Anchor Leg Mooring	L 16
Cb	Cobbles	J 8
cd	Candela	B 54
CG	Coastguard	T 10, 11
Ch	Church	E 10.1
Chy	Chimney	E 22
cm	Centimetre(s)	B 43
Co	Coral	J 10, K 16
† Consol	Consol Beacon	S 13
Cy	Clay	J 3

D		
DGPS	Differential Global Positioning System	S51
Dia	Diaphone	R 11
Dir	Direction light	P 30, 31
dm	Decimetre(s)	B 42
Dn, Dns	Dolphin(s)	F 20
DW	Deep Water route	M 27, N 12.4
dwt	Dead Weight Tonnage	
DZ	Danger Zone	Q 50

E		
E	East	B 10
ED	Existence Doubtful	I 1
Explos	Explosive	R 10
exting	Extinguished	P 55

F		
f	Fine	J 30
F	Fixed	P 10.1
FFl	Fixed and Flashing	P 10.10
Fl	Flashing	P 10.4
Fla	Flare stack	L 11
Fog Det Lt	Fog detector light	P 62
FS	Flagstaff, flagpole	E 27
ft	Foot/feet	B 47

G		
G	Gravel	J 6
G	Green	P 11.3, Q 2
GPS	Global Positioning System	
grt	Gross Register Tonnage	
GT	Gross Tonnage	

H		
h	Hard	J 39
h	Hour	B 49
H	Helicopter	T 1.4
hor	Horizontally disposed	P 15

I		
INT	International	A 2, T 21
Intens	Intensified	P 46
IQ	Interrupted quick	P 10.6
Iso	Isophase	P 10.3
IUQ	Interrupted ultra quick	P 10.8
IVQ	Interrupted very quick	P 10.7

K		
km	Kilometre(s)	B 40
kn	Knot(s)	B 52

L		
LANBY	Large Automatic Navigational Buoy	P 6, Q 26
LASH	Lighter Aboard Ship	G 184
Lat	Latitude	B 1
Ldg	Leading	P 20.3
LFl	Long-flashing	P 10.5
Lndg	Landing for boats	F 17
LNG	Liquefied Natural Gas	G 185
Long	Longitude	B 2
LPG	Liquefied Petroleum Gas	G 186
Lt	Light	P 1

M		
m	Medium	J 31
m	Metre(s)	B 41
m	Minute(s) of time	B 50
M	Mud	J 2
M	International Nautical mile(s) (1852 m) or sea mile(s)	B 45
min	Minute(s) of time	B 50
Mk	Mark	Q 101
mm	Millimetre(s)	B 44
Mo	Morse Code	P 10.9, R 20
Mon	Monument	E 24
MR	Marine Reserve	N 22.3

N		
N	North	B 9
NE	North-east	B 13
No	Number	N 12.2
NT	Net Tonnage	
NW	North-west	B 15

W International Abbreviations

O			
Obscd	Obscured	P 43	
Obstn	Obstruction	K 40-43, L 43	
Oc	Occulting	P 10.2	
occas	Occasional	P 50	
ODAS	Ocean Data Acquisition System	Q 58	
Or	Orange	P 11.7, Q 3	
P			
P	Pebbles	J 7	
PA	Position approximate	B 7	
PD	Position doubtful	B 8	
priv	Private	P 65, Q 70	
Prod Well	Submerged production well	L 20	
PSSA	Particularly Sensitive Sea Area	N 22.4	
Pyl	Pylon	D 26	
Q			
Q	Quick	P 10.6	
R			
R	Coast radio stations QTG service	S 15	
R	Red	P 11.2, Q 3	
R	Rock	J 9, K 15	
Ra	Radar	M 31, 32, S 1	
Racon	Radar transponder beacon	S 3.1-3.6	
† RC	Circular marine radiobeacon	S 10	
† RD	Directional radiobeacon	S 11	
Ref	Refuge	Q 124, T 14	
Rep	Reported, but not confirmed	I 3.1	
RG	Radio direction-finding station	S 14	
RoRo	Roll-on, Roll-off Ferry (RoRo Terminal)	F 50	
Ru	Ruin	D 8, E 25.2, F 33	
† RW	Rotating-pattern radiobeacon	S 12	
S			
S	Sand	J 1	
s	Second(s) of time	B 51, P 12	
S	South	B 11	
SALM	Single Anchor Leg Mooring	L 12	
SBM	Single Buoy Mooring	L 16	
SD	Sounding doubtful	I 2	
SE	South-east	B 14	
sec	Second(s) of time	B 51	
sf	Stiff	J 36	
Sh	Shells (skeletal remains)	J 11	
Si	Silt	J 4	
Sig	Signal	T 25.2	
SMt	Seamount	O 33	
so	Soft	J 35	
Sp	(Church) spire	E 10.3	
SPM	Single Point Mooring	L 12	
SS	Signal station	T 20-36	
St	Stones	J 5	
SW	South-west	B 16	
sy	Sticky	J 34	

T			
t	Ton(s), Tonne(s) or tonnage	B 53, F 53	
temp	Temporary	P 54	
Tr	Tower	E 10.2, 20	
U			
ULCC	Ultra Large Crude Carrier	G 188	
UQ	Ultra Quick	P 10.8	
UTC	Universal Time Co-ordinated		
UTM	Universal Transverse Mercator		
V			
v	Volcanic	J 37	
vert	Vertically disposed	P 15	
Vi	Violet	P 11.5	
VLCC	Very Large Crude Carrier	G 187	
VQ	Very Quick	P 10.7	
VTS	Vessel Traffic Service		
W			
W	West	B 12	
W	White	P 11.1, Q 130.5	
Wd	Weed	J 13.1	
Well	Wellhead	L 21	
WGS	World Geodetic System	S 50	
Whis	Whistle	R 15	
Wk; Wks	Wreck(s)	K 20-30	
Y			
Y	Amber	P 11.8	
Y	Orange	P 11.7	
Y	Yellow	P 11.6, Q 3	

See also Section V for Abbreviations of principal English and non-English terms, and Section W for International Abbreviations.

NOTES